LISA NIESCHLAG ★ LARS WENTRUP

NEW YORK
Christmas

PHOTOGRAPHY

LISA NIESCHLAG AND JULIA CAWLEY

CONTENTS

CHRISTMAS BAKING
Cookies, sweets & brownies

WINTER BRUNCH
Pancakes, bread & bagels

HAPPY HOLIDAYS
Burgers, soul food & cakes

CHRISTMAS DINNER
Starters, main dishes & desserts

NEW YEAR'S EVE
Appetisers, popcorn & drinks

Stories

THE AIR IS FULL OF ANTICIPATION...

When an icy wind sweeps through the streets of New York in the early days of December and plumes of white steam rise from the manhole covers in the ground, it usually doesn't take long before cold, moist air from the Great Lakes brings the first snow of the season to the city. Suddenly there are snowflakes dancing through the streets, and in the blink of an eye this great city turns into a winter wonderland. Time seems to stand still and New York business seems to hold its breath just for a moment. Anticipation takes hold on people's faces. As snow settles on the Big Apple like glittering fairy dust, the city starts to resemble the famous New York snow domes tourists love to take home as souvenirs.

Visitors from all over the world flock to the city year after year to enjoy New York's famous Christmas shopping or to don ice skates for a few rounds in Central Park. Gliding across the rink set against the wonderful backdrop of the city skyline, defying gravity, they share a sense of magic and unlimited possibility. In the pre-Christmas weeks, the city dresses up for its residents and tourists: this is when New York sparkles more than at any other time of the year, intoxicating locals and visitors alike with a sea of thousands of colourful lights and illuminated Christmas trees.

The ebb and flow between the pulsating power of the city and the magical spirit of the Christmas season is both thrilling and fascinating – not only along Broadway, but also in quiet side streets, in small, cosy, charmingly decorated cafés and even on enchanted benches in Central Park, where Julia Cawley loves to sit, enjoy the moment and simply watch time go by. Julia, a photographer who lives and works in New York, again and again finds herself drawn to the city as the focus of her work, creating a homage to this ever-changing metropolis.

New York's many-faceted character is also reflected in its food culture, and of course both the city and its surroundings have a lot to offer to gourmets, especially at this, the most beautiful time of the year. We have found just the recipes to bring this atmosphere to you. We have adapted sugar and butter quantities to local tastes and styled and photographed these sweet, savoury and sparkling delicacies with a great deal of love and care.

Join us on an exciting trip, immerse yourself in the stories of a mesmerising city, and taste the essence of what makes New York so unique in the world.

Lisa Nieschlag and Lars Wentrup

LISA NIESCHLAG

LARS WENTRUP

JULIA CAWLEY

AUGGIE WREN'S
Christmas Story

Paul Auster

I heard this story from Auggie Wren. Since Auggie doesn't come off too well in it, at least not as well as he'd like to, he's asked me not to use his real name. Other than that, the whole business about the lost wallet and the blind woman and the Christmas dinner is just as he told it to me.

Auggie and I have known each other for close to eleven years now. He works behind the counter of a cigar store on Court Street in downtown Brooklyn, and since it's the only store that carries the little Dutch cigars I like to smoke, I go in there fairly often. For a long time, I didn't give much thought to Auggie Wren. He was the strange little man who wore a hooded blue sweatshirt and sold me cigars and magazines, the impish, wisecracking character who always had something funny to say about the weather, the Mets or the politicians in Washington, and that was the extent of it.

But then one day several years ago he happened to be looking through a magazine in the store, and he stumbled across a review of one of my books. He knew it was me because a photograph accompanied the review, and after that things changed between us. I was no longer just another customer to Auggie, I had become a distinguished person. Most people couldn't care less about books and writers, but it turned out that Auggie considered himself an artist. Now that he had cracked the secret of who I was, he embraced me

as an ally, a confidant, a brother-in-arms. To tell the truth, I found it rather embarrassing. Then, almost inevitably, a moment came when he asked if I would be willing to look at his photographs. Given his enthusiasm and goodwill, there didn't seem any way I could turn him down.

God knows what I was expecting. At the very least, it wasn't what Auggie showed me the next day. In a small, windowless room at the back of the store, he opened a cardboard box and pulled out twelve identical black photo albums. This was his life's work, he said, and it didn't take him more than five minutes a day to do it. Every morning for the past twelve years, he had stood on the corner of Atlantic

Avenue and Clinton Street at precisely seven o'clock and had taken a single color photograph of precisely the same view. The project now ran to more than four thousand photographs. Each album represented a different year, and all the pictures were laid out in sequence, from January 1 to December 31, with the dates carefully recorded under each one.

As I flipped through the albums and began to study Auggie's work, I didn't know what to think. My first impression was that it was the oddest, most bewildering thing I had ever seen. All the pictures were the same. The whole project was a numbing onslaught of repetition, the same street and the same buildings over and over again, an unrelenting delirium

of redundant images. I couldn't think of anything to say to Auggie, so I continued turning pages, nodding my head in feigned appreciation. Auggie himself seemed unperturbed, watching me with a broad smile on his face, but after I'd been at it for several minutes, he suddenly interrupted and said, "You're going too fast. You'll never get it if you don't slow down."

He was right, of course. If you don't take the time to look, you'll never manage to see anything. I picked up another album and forced myself to go more deliberately. I paid closer attention to the details, took note of the shifts in weather, watched for the changing angles of light as the seasons advanced. Eventually I was able to detect subtle differences in the traffic flow, to anticipate the rhythm of the different days (the commotion of workday mornings, the relative stillness of weekends, the contrast between Saturdays and Sundays). And then, little by little, I began to recognize the faces of the people in the background, the passers-by on their way to work, the same people in the same spot every morning, living an instant of their lives in the field of Auggie's camera.

Once I got to know them, I began to study their postures, the way they carried themselves from one morning to the next, trying to discover their moods from these surface indications, as if I could imagine stories for them, as if I could penetrate the invisible dramas locked inside their bodies. I picked up another album. I was no longer bored, no longer puzzled as I had been at first. Auggie was photographing time, I realized, both natural time and human time, and he was doing it by planting himself in one tiny corner of the world and willing it to be his own, by standing guard in the space he had chosen for himself. As he watched me pore over his work, Auggie continued to smile with pleasure. Then, almost as if he'd been reading my thoughts, he began to recite a line from Shakespeare. "Tomorrow and tomorrow and tomorrow," he muttered under his breath,

"time creeps on its petty pace." I understood then that he knew exactly what he was doing.

That was more than two thousand pictures ago. Since that day, Auggie and I have discussed his work many times, but it was only last week that I learned how he acquired his camera and started taking pictures in the first place. That was the subject of the story he told me, and I'm still struggling to make sense of it.

Earlier that same week, a man from the *New York Times* called me and asked if I would be willing to write a short story that would appear in the paper on Christmas morning. My first impulse was to say no, but the man was very charming and persistent, and by the end of the conversation I told him I would give it a try. The moment I hung up the phone, however, I fell into a deep panic. What did I know about Christmas? I asked myself. What did I know about writing short stories on commission?

I spent the next several days in despair, warring with the ghosts of Dickens, O. Henry and other masters of the Yuletide spirit. The very phrase "Christmas story" had unpleasant associations for me, evoking dreadful outpourings of hypocritical mush and treacle. Even at their best, Christmas stories were no more than wish-fulfillment dreams, fairy tales for adults, and I'd be damned if I'd ever allowed myself to write something like that. And yet, how could anyone propose to write an unsentimental Christmas story? It was a contradiction in terms, an impossibility, an out-and-out conundrum. One might just as well try to imagine a racehorse without legs, or a sparrow without wings.

I got nowhere. On Thursday I went out for a long walk, hoping the air would clear my head. Just past noon, I stopped in at the cigar store to replenish my supply, and there was Auggie, standing behind the counter as always. He asked me how I was. Without really meaning to, I found myself unburdening my troubles to him. "A Christmas story?" he said after I had finished. "Is that all? If you buy me lunch, my friend, I'll tell you the best Christmas story you ever heard. And I guarantee that every word of it is true."

We walked down the block to Jack's, a cramped and boisterous delicatessen with good pastrami sandwiches and photographs of old Dodgers teams hanging on the walls. We found a table in the back, ordered our food, and then Auggie launched into his story.

"It was the summer of seventy-two," he said. "A kid came in one morning and started stealing things from the store. He must have been about nineteen or twenty, and I don't think I've ever seen a more pathetic shoplifter in my life. He's standing by the rack of paperbacks along the far wall and stuffing books into the pockets of his raincoat. It was crowded around the counter just then, so I didn't see him at first. But once I noticed what he was up to, I started to shout. He took off like a jackrabbit, and by the time I managed to get out from behind the counter, he was already tearing down Atlantic Avenue. I chased after him for about half a block, and then I gave up. He'd dropped something along the way, and since I didn't feel like running any more, I bent down to see what it was.

"It turned out to be his wallet. There wasn't any money inside, but his driver's license was there along with three or four snapshots. I suppose I could have called the cops and had him arrested. I had his name and address from the license, but I felt kind of sorry for him. He was just a measly little punk, and once I looked at those pictures in his wallet, I couldn't bring myself to feel very angry at him. Robert Goodwin. That was his name. In one of the pictures, I remember, he was standing with his arm around his mother or grandmother. In another one he was sitting there at age nine or ten dressed in a baseball uniform with a big smile on his face. I just didn't have the heart.

He was probably on dope now, I figured. A poor kid from Brooklyn without much going for him, and who cared about a couple of trashy paperbacks anyway?

"So I held on to the wallet. Every once in a while I'd get a little urge to send it back to him, but I kept delaying and never did anything about it. Then Christmas rolls around and I'm stuck with nothing to do. The boss usually invites me over to his house to spend the day, but that year he and his family were down in Florida visiting relatives. So I'm sitting in my apartment that morning feeling a little sorry for myself, and then I see Robert Goodwin's wallet lying on a shelf in the kitchen. I figure what the hell, why not do something nice for once, and I put on my coat and go out to return the wallet in person.

"The address was over in Boerum Hill, somewhere in the projects. It was freezing out that day, and I remember getting lost a few times trying to find the right building. Everything looks the same in that place, and you keep going over the same ground thinking you're somewhere else. Anyway, I finally get to the apartment I'm looking for and ring the bell. Nothing happens. I assume no one's there, but I try again just to make sure. I wait a little longer, and just when I'm about to give up, I hear someone shuffling to the door. An old woman's voice asks who's there, and I say I'm looking for Robert Goodwin. 'Is that you, Robert?' the old woman says, and then she undoes about fifteen locks and opens the door.

"She has to be at least eighty, maybe ninety years old, and the first thing I notice about her is that she's blind. 'I knew you'd come, Robert,' she says. 'I knew you wouldn't forget your Granny Ethel on Christmas.' And then she opens her arms as if she's about to hug me.

"I didn't have much time to think, you understand. I had to say something real fast, and before I knew what was happening, I could hear the words coming out of my mouth. 'That's right, Granny Ethel,' I said.

'I came back to see you on Christmas.' Don't ask me why I did it. I don't have any idea. Maybe I didn't want to disappoint her or something, I don't know. It just came out that way, and then this old woman was suddenly hugging me there in front of the door, and I was hugging her back.

"I didn't exactly say I was her grandson. Not in so many words, at least, but that was the implication. I wasn't trying to trick her, though. It was like a game we'd both decided to play - without having to discuss the rules. I mean, that woman knew I wasn't her grandson Robert. She was old and dotty, but she wasn't so far gone that she couldn't tell the difference between a stranger and her own flesh and blood. But it made her happy to pretend, and since I had nothing better to do anyway, I was happy to go along with her.

"So we went into the apartment and spent the day together. The place was a real dump, I might add, but what else can you expect from a blind woman who does her own housekeeping? Every time she asked me a question about how I was, I would lie to her. I told her I found a good job working in a cigar store, I told her I was about to get married, I told her a hundred pretty stories, and she made like she believed every one of them. 'That's fine, Robert,' she would say, nodding her head and smiling. 'I always knew things would work out for you.'

"After a while, I started getting pretty hungry. There didn't seem to be much food in the house, so I went out to a store in the neighborhood and brought back a mess of stuff. A precooked chicken, vegetable soup, a bucket of potato salad, a chocolate cake, all kinds of things. Ethel had a couple of bottles of wine stashed in her bedroom, and so between us we managed to put together a fairly decent Christmas dinner. We both got a little tipsy from the wine, I remember, and after the meal was over we went out to sit in the living room, where the chairs were more comfortable. I had to take a pee, so I excused myself and went to the bathroom down the hall. That's where things took yet another turn. It was ditsy enough doing my little jig

as Ethel's grandson, but what I did next was positively crazy, and I've never forgiven myself for it.

"I go into the bathroom, and stacked up against the wall next to the shower, I see a pile of six or seven cameras. Brand-new thirty-five-millimeter cameras, still in their boxes, top-quality merchandise. I figure this is the work of the real Robert, a storage place for one of his recent hauls. I've never taken a picture in my life, and I've certainly never stolen anything, but the moment I see those cameras sitting in the bathroom, I decide I want one of them for myself. Just like that. And without even stopping to think about it, I tuck one of those boxes under my arm and go back to the living room. "I couldn't have been gone for more than a few minutes, but in that time Granny Ethel had fallen asleep in her chair. Too much Chianti, I suppose. I went into the kitchen to wash the dishes, and she slept on through the whole racket, snoring like a baby. There didn't seem any point in disturbing her, so I decided to leave. I couldn't even write her a note to say goodbye, seeing that she was blind and all, and so I just left. I put her grandson's wallet on the table, picked up the camera again, and walked out of the apartment. And that's the end of the story."

"Did you ever go back to see her?" I asked.

"Once," he said. "About three or four months later. I felt so bad about stealing the camera, I hadn't even used it yet. I finally made up my mind to return it, but Ethel wasn't there anymore. I don't know what happened to her, but someone else had moved into the apartment, and he couldn't tell me where she was."

"She probably died."

"Yeah, probably."

"Which means that she spent her last Christmas with you."

"I guess so. I never thought of it that way."

"It was a good deed, Auggie. It was a nice thing you did for her."

"I lied to her, and then I stole from her. I don't see how you can call that a good deed."

"You made her happy. And the camera was stolen anyway. It's not as if the person you took it from really owned it."

"Anything for art, eh, Paul?"

"I wouldn't say that. But at least you've put the camera to good use."

"And now you've got your Christmas story, don't you?"

"Yes," I said. "I suppose I do."

I paused for a moment, studying Auggie as a wicked grin spread across his face. I couldn't be sure, but the look in his eyes at that moment was so mysterious, so fraught with the glow of some inner delight, that it suddenly occurred to me that he had made the whole thing up. I was about to ask him if he'd been putting me on, but then I realized he would never tell. I had been tricked into believing him, and that was the only thing that mattered. As long as there's one person to believe it, there's no story that can't be true.

"You're an ace, Auggie," I said. "Thanks for being so helpful."

"Any time," he answered, still looking at me with that maniacal light in his eyes. "After all, if you can't share your secrets with your friends, what kind of a friend are you?"

"I guess I owe you one."

"No you don't. Just put it down the way I told it to you, and you don't owe me a thing."

"Except the lunch."

"That's right. Except the lunch."

I returned Auggie's smile with a smile of my own, and then I called out to the waiter and asked for the check.

CHRISTMAS BAKING

COOKIES, SWEETS & BROWNIES

CHRISTMAS MACADAMIA COOKIES

Not everybody loves macadamias, perhaps because they start to turn rancid quite quickly and then taste stale. Fresh macadamia nuts, however, have a deliciously subtle, buttery flavour and give our cookies the perfect crunch. Macadamias are native to Australia's tropical rain forests and have been enjoyed as a particularly rich source of food by Aboriginal Australians for centuries. Today they are so popular that sometimes there are macadamia shortages, as these nuts are quite tricky to grow and process. No wonder the macadamia is called the "queen of nuts"!

★ INGREDIENTS

Makes about 16

40 g (1½ oz/¼ cup) macadamia nuts
40 g (1½ oz/¼ cup) blanched almonds
1–2 tbsp honey
100 g (3½ oz) high-quality white chocolate
190 g (6¾ oz) flour
1 tsp baking powder
¼ tsp cinnamon
1 pinch salt
130 g (4½ oz) butter, softened
60 g (2¼ oz) brown sugar
1 egg

Coarsely chop the macadamia nuts and almonds and dry-roast lightly in a frying pan. Add the honey and allow the nuts and almonds to caramelise gently. Set the pan aside and allow to cool.

Chop the chocolate. Combine the flour, baking powder, cinnamon and salt in a mixing bowl. In another bowl, whisk the butter with the sugar until creamy. Add the egg and whisk to combine. Stir the dry ingredients into the mixture a little at a time. Finally fold in the chopped, toasted macadamias, almonds and chopped chocolate using a spatula. Cover the bowl and chill for 30 minutes.

Make sure to preheat the oven in time to 180°C (350°F/Gas mark 4). Line a baking tray with baking paper. Shape the dough into balls about 3 cm (1¼ inches) in diameter. Set the balls on the prepared baking tray about 3 cm (1¼ inches) apart and press to flatten gently. Bake the cookies in the preheated oven for about 15–17 minutes. (Move the tray to the highest rack in the oven after about 10 minutes if the cookies turn too dark on the bottom.) Leave the cookies on a rack to cool.

BLUEBERRY BROWNIES

Brownie recipes often ask for a lot of butter or nuts to be added to the dough to make them deliciously moist and chewy, but blueberries make for a healthier alternative. The blueberries folded into the dough not only give these brownies a delightfully fruity flavour, but also make them irresistibly fudgy.

With baking paper, carefully line a rectangular pan (about 20 x 24 cm/8 inches x 9½ inches). Break the two types of chocolate into pieces. Add to a heat-proof bowl together with the butter and melt over a double boiler, stirring occasionally. Set aside to cool.

Preheat the oven to 180°C (350°F/Gas mark 4). Dissolve the instant espresso in 2 tablespoons hot water. Combine the eggs, sugar and vanilla sugar in a mixing bowl and whisk until foamy. Add the espresso, flour and salt and mix to combine, then stir in the cooled, melted chocolate. Gently fold in the blueberries with a spatula.

Spread the batter evenly across the pan and bake in the preheated oven for 30–35 minutes. Use a toothpick to test for doneness! Allow to cool in the pan.

Melt the semi-sweet cooking chocolate and butter in a double boiler, stirring occasionally. Spread the frosting evenly across the brownies. Leave to set and then cut into pieces about 5–6 cm (2¼ inches) in size.

INGREDIENTS

Makes about 12

For the dough:
80 g (2¾ oz) high-quality
semi-sweet chocolate
80 g (2¾ oz) high-quality
milk chocolate
125 g (4½ oz) butter
1 tbsp instant espresso powder
4 eggs
140 g (5 oz) raw cane sugar
(golden granulated sugar)
1-2 tsp vanilla sugar
120 g (4¼ oz) flour
1 pinch salt
300 g (10½ oz) frozen
blueberries, defrosted

For the frosting:
150 g (5½ oz) semi-sweet
cooking chocolate
50 g (1¾ oz) butter

SALTY PEANUT BUTTER ROUNDS

Peanut butter cookies are very popular in the United States, where people often enjoy them together with a glass of milk in the afternoon. They also make great gifts and are perfect for bringing along to an afternoon or morning tea. We lined an old cookie tin with parchment paper and then wrapped the peanut butter rounds in festive Christmas cellophane. Stored in a dry place away from light, these cookies will keep for at least two weeks.

Add the butter, peanut butter and both types of sugar to a mixing bowl and whisk until creamy, then stir in the egg. Combine the flour with the baking powder and add the mixture gradually to make a soft, pliable dough.

Preheat the oven to 180°C (350°F/Gas mark 4) and line a tray with baking paper. Coarsely chop the peanuts and place them on a shallow plate. Form the dough into walnut-sized balls. Dip one half of the balls into the chopped peanuts and then place on the baking tray. Flatten the cookies slightly. Bake the cookies for about 14–18 minutes, depending on size.

★
INGREDIENTS

Makes about 16–18

100 g (3½ oz) butter, softened
120 g (4¼ oz) crunchy
peanut butter
100 g (3½ oz) brown sugar
1-2 tsp vanilla sugar
1 egg
220 g (7¾ oz) flour
2 tsp baking powder

Also:
100 g (3½ oz) peanuts,
roasted and salted

CANDY CANE CUPCAKES

Numerous legends are wrapped around the origins of the famous red and white, peppermint-flavoured candy canes. According to one story, it was an elder of Cologne Cathedral who had candy canes first made in the 17th century to give them to children, as a reward if they served at the altar or had behaved well in church. The canes are modelled after a shepherd's crook to remind people of the shepherds who came to pay homage to Jesus at Bethlehem. This is also why candy canes were traditionally shared out during nativity plays. Both nativity plays and candy canes spread across Europe and eventually also to the United States, where candy canes are still an important Christmas symbol even today.

★ INGREDIENTS

Makes 8

For the dough:
150 g (5½ oz/1 cup) flour
2 tbsp cocoa powder
1½ tsp baking powder
1 pinch salt
100 g (3½ oz) butter
30 ml (1 fl oz) milk
2 eggs
100 g (3½ oz) caster
(superfine) sugar

For the frosting:
50 g (1¾ oz) butter, softened
150 g (5½ oz) cream cheese
(full fat)
350 g (12 oz) icing sugar
(confectioner's sugar)
1 tsp vanilla extract

Also:
3–4 candy canes, chopped

Preheat the oven to 180°C (350°F/Gas mark 4). For the dough, combine the flour, cocoa powder, baking powder and salt. Melt the butter in a small saucepan. Stir in the milk and allow to cool. Beat the eggs and sugar in another bowl until foamy. Whisk in the melted butter and then fold in the dry ingredients.

Line an 8-hole muffin tray with paper cup liners. Fill the liners about three quarters with dough and bake in a preheated oven for about 18 minutes. Use a toothpick to test for doneness! Allow the muffins to cool completely.

For the frosting, combine butter and cream cheese in a bowl. Gradually add the icing sugar. Stir in the vanilla extract. Spread the frosting over the cooled cupcakes with a knife; alternatively use a piping bag to pipe it on. Decorate with chopped candy cane.

WHOOPIE PIES

Our creamy pink filling is very easy to make without any artificial food colouring by simply using beetroot juice. Beetroot juice not only provides for an interesting dot of colour between the whoopie pie halves, but its flavour also harmonises perfectly with the dark, bitter chocolate.

★ INGREDIENTS

Makes about 15–17

For the dough:
140 g (5 oz) flour
20 g (¾ oz) cocoa powder
½ tsp baking powder
½ tsp cinnamon
1 pinch salt
65 g (2¼ oz) butter, softened
90 g (3¼ oz) caster
(superfine) sugar
1 egg, lightly beaten
1 tsp vanilla extract
125 ml (4 fl oz/½ cup)
buttermilk

For the filling:
125 g (4½ oz) butter, softened
250 g (9 oz/2 cups) icing sugar
(confectioner's sugar)
2–3 tsp beetroot (beet) juice
20 g (¾ oz) semi-sweet
chocolate, finely grated
2–3 tsp milk

For the dough, combine the flour, cocoa powder, baking powder, cinnamon and salt in a mixing bowl. Whisk butter and sugar in another bowl until fluffy. Gradually add the egg and vanilla extract, then alternate adding the flour mix and the buttermilk until you have a soft, fluffy dough.

Preheat the oven to 180°C (350°F/Gas mark 4). Line two trays with baking paper. Transfer the dough to a piping bag and pipe about 32 round heaps of dough (2.5–3 cm or 1 inch) onto the baking paper, spacing them a little apart. Bake the two trays for 12–14 minutes on the middle rack, one after the other, then leave to cool fully on a rack.

For the filling, whisk the butter until creamy, then gradually add the icing sugar to make a thick, light-coloured cream. Divide the cream between two bowls. Stir the beetroot juice into one half and combine the other half with the grated chocolate and milk. Place a dollop of each filling on the flat side of two whoopie halves. Combine the two halves and press together gently.

SNOWCAPS

These chocolate cookies with their dusting of white icing sugar bring the image of snow-covered mountains to mind, which is where their romantic name comes from.

★
INGREDIENTS

Makes about 15–18

100 g (3½ oz) high-quality
semi-sweet chocolate
(70% cocoa)
40 g (1½ oz) butter
2 eggs
60 g (2¼ oz) caster
(superfine) sugar
120 g (4¼ oz) flour
1 heaped tbsp cocoa powder
½ tsp cream of tartar powder
1 tsp cinnamon
1 pinch salt
Scraped out seeds of 1 vanilla pod
50 g (1¾ oz) icing sugar
(confectioner's sugar)

Coarsely chop the chocolate. Combine in a bowl with the butter and melt over a double boiler. Set aside and leave to cool.

Whisk the eggs and sugar until foamy. Combine the flour, cocoa powder, cream of tartar powder, cinnamon and salt in another bowl. Stir the cooled, liquid chocolate mass into the egg mass, then fold in the dry ingredients and scraped out vanilla seeds. Cover the bowl and chill for 2 hours.

Make sure to preheat the oven in time to 180°C (350°F/Gas mark 4). Line a tray with baking paper. Sieve the icing sugar into a shallow bowl. Shape the dough into walnut-sized balls and roll these generously in the icing sugar until they are thickly covered. Place the snowcaps onto the baking tray, setting them a little apart. Bake in the middle of the oven for about 13–15 minutes, depending on size, then leave on a rack to cool.

OAT COOKIES WITH CRANBERRIES AND ALMONDS

These traditional cookies are delicious at any time of the year, not just around Christmas. Oats give the cookies just the perfect amount of crunch and bite. If you cannot get enough of these cookies, but would like a little variety, add 1 tablespoon cocoa powder to the basic recipe or substitute other dried fruit for the cranberries.

★
INGREDIENTS

Makes about 24

100 g (3½ oz) butter, softened
90 g (3¼ oz) brown sugar
1-2 tsp vanilla sugar
100 g (3½ oz) spelt flour
1 tsp cream of tartar powder
1 pinch salt
1 egg
1 tbsp honey
90 g (3¼ oz) quick-cooking oats
50 g (1¾ oz) chopped almonds
75 g (2½ oz) dried cranberries

Combine butter, sugar and vanilla sugar in a mixing bowl and whisk until creamy. Combine the flour, cream of tartar powder and salt in another bowl. Add the dry ingredients to the butter mass together with the egg and honey, then stir in the oats, almonds and cranberries. Chill the dough for about 45 minutes.

Preheat the oven to 180°C (350°F/Gas mark 4) and line a tray with baking paper. Drop the mixture onto the tray in lots of 1 heaped teaspoon each. If you like, use your hands to shape the slightly sticky dough into balls to give the baked cookies a more even shape.

Transfer the tray to the preheated oven and bake for about 14–16 minutes until the cookies are golden brown. (You may want to move the tray to the highest rack after about 7–8 minutes if the cookies turn too dark on the bottom.) Leave on a rack to cool.

LEMON TARTLETS WITH PISTACHIO MERINGUE

★
INGREDIENTS

*Makes about 6 tartlets
(10 cm/4 inches each)*

For the dough:
90 g (3¼ oz) flour
50 g (1¾ oz) cream cheese
(full fat)
50 g (1¾ oz) butter, softened
40 g (1½ oz) icing sugar
(confectioner's sugar)
40 g (1½ oz) ground almonds
½ tsp cinnamon
1 pinch salt

For the lemon filling:
80 g (2¾ oz) cornflour
(cornstarch)
280 g (10 oz) caster
(superfine) sugar
100 ml (3½ fl oz) lemon juice
4 egg yolks
1 generous pinch of salt
Zest of 1 organic lemon, grated
50 g (1¾ oz) butter

For the meringue:
4 egg whites
220 g (7¾ oz) icing sugar
(confectioner's sugar)
2 handfuls of pistachios,
shelled and chopped

Also:
Butter and flour for the moulds
Flour for dusting the work surface

Add all the dough ingredients to a mixing bowl and knead well to combine. Cover with cling wrap and chill for at least 45 minutes.

Preheat the oven to 190°C (375°F/Gas mark 5). Butter 6 tartlet moulds and dust with flour. Roll out the pastry thinly on a lightly floured surface and cut out circles (about 13 cm/5 inches). Press the pastry rounds into the prepared moulds. Prick the bases with a fork and pre-bake them in the oven for 10–12 minutes. Leave to cool and reduce the oven temperature to 150°C (300°F/Gas mark 2).

For the filling: combine the cornflour, sugar and 200 ml (7 fl oz) water in a saucepan and whisk until smooth. Stir in the lemon juice, egg yolks and salt and heat. Simmer the mixture for about 8 minutes, stirring constantly, as the mass thickens considerably and burns easily. Add the lemon zest and butter, remove the saucepan from the heat and leave the lemon filling to cool.

For the meringue: whisk the egg whites, gradually adding the icing sugar. Beat for several minutes until the egg whites form small, glossy peaks. Divide the lemon filling among the bases. Transfer the meringue mass into a piping bag and pipe domes of meringue onto the fillings. Alternatively spread the meringue out with a spoon. Sprinkle with pistachios and bake the tartlets in the oven for 15–20 minutes.

DOUGHNUTS WITH ORANGE VANILLA FROSTING

Doughnuts come in a huge range of varieties, decorated with icing, hundreds and thousands, nut brittle or chocolate. Oil for deep-frying doughnuts must have a temperature of about 170°C, which is why preparing these delicacies requires a little bit of skill and care. But don't let yourself be deterred by this – after all, fresh home-made doughnuts are simply the best!

★
INGREDIENTS

Makes about 10–12

For the dough:
250 g (9 oz) flour, plus a little
more if needed
1 tsp dried yeast
1 pinch salt
30 g (1 oz) caster
(superfine) sugar
1-2 tsp vanilla sugar
1 egg
75 ml (2¼ fl oz) lukewarm milk
40 g (1½ oz) butter, softened

For the frosting (icing):
150 g (5½ oz) icing sugar
(confectioner's sugar)
2–3 tbsp orange juice
1 tsp vanilla extract
A little zest from
1 organic orange (optional)

Also:
Flour for dusting the
work surface
Vegetable oil for deep-frying
(about 750 ml/26 fl oz/3 cups
depending on the size of
the saucepan)

For the dough, combine the flour, yeast, salt, sugar and vanilla sugar in a mixing bowl. Add the egg, milk and butter and knead everything for at least 5 minutes to make a smooth, pliable dough. Add a little more flour if the dough seems too sticky and soft. Cover the bowl with cling wrap and leave the dough to rise for about 1 hour.

Roll out the dough about 1.5 cm (⅝ inch) thick on a lightly floured surface. Use a cookie cutter to cut out rounds about 6 cm (2½ inches) in diameter, then use a 2 cm (¾ inch) cutter to cut out circles from the middle of each round. Alternatively use a large drinking glass and small shot glass for cutting the dough. Knead leftover dough together and cut out more doughnuts. Place the doughnuts onto trays lined with baking paper and leave to rise for about another 15 minutes.

Add oil to a medium-sized, deep pan to come up about 4 cm (1½ inches). Heat to 170°C (325°F/Gas mark 3). Slide the doughnuts into the hot oil using a skimming ladle and bake until golden all around, turning once. This should take about 1–1½ minutes per side. Remove the doughnuts from the oil and set them on kitchen paper to drain excess oil and cool.

For the frosting, combine all ingredients in a bowl. Dip the doughnuts into the frosting to cover the tops and leave them to dry.

WE WISH YOU A MERRY CHRISTMAS

We wish you a Merry Christmas,
We wish you a Merry Christmas,
And a Happy New Year!

Good tidings we bring
To you and your king
Good tidings for Christmas
And a Happy New Year!

Now bring us some figgy pudding,
Now bring us some figgy pudding,
Now bring us some figgy pudding,
And bring some out here!

For we all like figgy pudding,
We all like figgy pudding,
We all like figgy pudding,
So bring some out here!

And we won't go until we've got some,
We won't go until we've got some,
We won't go until we've got some,
So bring some out here!

WINTER BRUNCH

PANCAKES, BREAD & BAGELS

PANCAKES WITH MAPLE SYRUP AND CINNAMON BUTTER

In the USA, pancakes are a favourite breakfast dish. Served with this maple syrup and cinnamon butter, they are irresistibly moist and festive. If you like, you can add a little thinly sliced apple on top while frying the pancakes.

INGREDIENTS

Serves 3–4
(about 14 small pancakes)

For the dough:
2 eggs
120 g (4¼ oz) flour
30 g (1 oz) caster
(superfine) sugar
2 tsp cream of tartar powder
200 ml (7 fl oz) buttermilk
40 ml (1¼ fl oz) milk
20 g (¾ oz) butter, melted
1 pinch salt

*For the maple syrup
and cinnamon butter:*
120 g (4¼ oz) butter, softened
2 tbsp maple syrup
½ tsp cinnamon

Also:
Butter for frying
60 g (2¼ oz) pecan nuts,
whole or coarsely chopped

Add the butter, maple syrup and cinnamon to a mixing bowl. Whisk until creamy and set aside.

Separate the eggs for the batter. Combine the flour, sugar and cream of tartar powder in a mixing bowl. Create a well in the centre. Add the egg yolks, buttermilk, milk and butter and whisk to make a smooth batter. Add the salt to the egg whites and beat until stiff. Gently fold the egg whites into the batter. Set the batter aside to rest for about 15 minutes.

Preheat the oven to 90°C (194°F/Gas mark 5). Melt a little butter in a frying pan over medium heat. Add 2–3 small ladlefuls of batter to the pan at a time. Fry for about 2 minutes, then flip the pancakes over and fry on the other side for another minute or until golden brown. Continue with the remaining batter. Transfer the cooked pancakes to a plate and keep them warm in the oven. Once you have used up all the batter, divide the pancakes among plates, sprinkle with pecan nuts and serve with maple syrup and cinnamon butter.

SWEET BREAD WITH ORANGE ZEST

In our home, this light bread just seems to vanish off the table in no time, but in case you do have stale leftovers, it also makes the perfect base for bread and butter puddings. Alternatively fry slices of dry bread in a pan with a little butter to allow the sugar in the bread to caramelise. We love it!

INGREDIENTS

Makes 1 loaf

500 g (1 lb 2 oz) flour
2 tsp dried yeast
50 g (1¾ oz) sugar
½ tsp salt
¼ tsp cinnamon
275 ml (9½ fl oz) lukewarm milk
50 g (1¾ oz) butter, softened
Zest of ½ orange (organic)
About 50 g (1¾ oz) raisins

Also:
Butter and flour for the loaf pan
Flour for dusting the
work surface
Milk for brushing

Combine the flour, yeast, sugar and salt in a mixing bowl. Add the milk, butter and orange zest and knead everything for at least 8 minutes to make a smooth, pliable dough. Add the raisins, if using, and carefully fold them in. Cover the bowl with cling wrap and leave the dough to rise for about 2 hours.

Butter a loaf tin and dust with flour. Dust your benchtop with flour. Remove the dough from the bowl and shape it into a loaf. Transfer the dough to the loaf tin. Cover with cling wrap and leave to rise for another 45 minutes.

Make sure to preheat the oven in time to 220°C (425°F/Gas mark 7). Place a small bowl of water on the bottom of the oven. Cut the loaf diagonally with a sharp knife every 2 cm (¾ inch) and brush with a little milk.

Transfer the loaf tin to the oven. Remove the bowl of water after 10 minutes and reduce the temperature to 200°C (400°F/Gas mark 6). Move the tin to the lowest rack and continue to bake for about another 30 minutes. If the surface gets too dark after only half of the baking time, cover the loaf with aluminium foil. Remove the loaf tin from the oven. Carefully flip it over to remove the loaf from the tin and leave on a rack to cool.

BACON & EGGS

This is a different take on bacon & eggs: baby spinach, feta and eggs are served in a shell of bacon, baked to perfection in muffin tins. Make sure to use small eggs – otherwise you may get too much egg white running into the muffin moulds. Small eggs should give you a shell of delectably crispy bacon.

INGREDIENTS

Serves 4

120 g (4¼ oz) baby spinach
1 garlic clove
1 shallot
2 tbsp olive oil
1 pinch ground nutmeg
Salt, pepper
100 g (3½ oz/⅔ cup) feta
4 large Swiss brown mushrooms
2 sprigs flat-leaf parsley
About 16 slices bacon or
pancetta
4 eggs

Pick through the baby spinach. Wash and spin dry. Peel the garlic and shallot. Mince the garlic and finely dice the shallot. Heat 1 tablespoon olive oil in a frying pan. Add the minced garlic and diced shallot and sweat for a few minutes. Add the spinach and allow to wilt for about 3–4 minutes. Season with nutmeg and a little salt and pepper. Once cool enough to handle, squeeze out excess moisture.

Dice the feta. Trim, quarter and slice the mushrooms. Rinse the parsley, shake off excess water and pick off the leaves.

Preheat the oven to 180°C, fan-forced (350°F/Gas mark 4). Line 4 holes of a muffin tin with 4 slices of bacon each. Leave the edges to overhang and make sure that the bottoms are fully covered. Place 1 tablespoon of the spinach mix each on the bacon. Press in gently. Top with a little diced feta. Carefully crack the eggs and slide one egg each into the moulds. Place the muffin tin into the preheated oven and bake for 14–18 minutes until the egg whites have set.

Meanwhile, heat the remaining olive oil in the same pan and fry the sliced mushrooms for about 4–5 minutes. Season with salt and pepper. Stir in the parsley and remove the pan from the heat. Carefully lift the cooked eggs from the muffin tin and divide them among plates. Season with pepper and serve with the mushrooms on the side.

HERBED MONKEY BREAD

In the USA, traditional monkey bread is prepared with cinnamon and served as a sweet breakfast dish. Our savoury version not only tastes amazing, but also makes a perfect centre piece for any breakfast or brunch table with many guests. It is not quite clear how monkey bread came by its name: some say that it is named after the fruits of the African baobab or monkey bread tree, which look a little like these dough balls...

Put the flour in a large mixing bowl and combine with the yeast, sugar and salt. Add the milk, egg and butter and knead everything for about 5 minutes to make a smooth, pliable dough. Add a little more milk if the dough seems too dry and firm. Cover the bowl and leave the dough to rise for about 1 hour or until it has doubled in volume.

Meanwhile, make the topping. Combine the thyme, garlic salt, oregano, rosemary and pepper, chopped almonds, parmesan and paprika powder in a small bowl.

Divide the risen dough into 24 portions of about 23–25 grams (1 oz) and shape into small balls. Roll 6 balls at a time first in the melted butter and then in the topping. Layer the balls in the buttered kuglof tin, leaving a little space between them to allow them to rise. Cover the tin and leave the dough to rise for another 45 minutes.

Make sure to preheat the oven in time to 180°C (350°F/Gas mark 4). Bake the monkey bread on the middle rack for about 30 minutes. Cover the tin with aluminium foil if the top dough balls turn too dark. Remove the tin from the oven and set aside to cool before removing the bread from the tin.

INGREDIENTS

For 1 kuglof (ring mould) tin (20–22 cm/8-8½ inches)

For the dough:
350 g (12 oz) flour
1¼ tsp dry yeast
20 g (¾ oz) sugar
½ tsp salt
125 ml (4 fl oz) lukewarm milk, plus a little extra if needed
1 egg
25 g (1 oz) butter, softened, plus a little extra for the tin

For the topping:
2 tsp dried thyme
1 pinch garlic salt
1 tsp dried oregano
1 tsp dried rosemary
1 pinch pepper
4 tsp chopped almonds
1 tbsp parmesan, grated
½ tsp paprika powder
25 g (1 oz) butter, melted

CORNBREAD MUFFINS WITH PARMESAN AND SESAME

These delicious muffins, which are a different take on conventional cornbread, make an excellent side dish for any salad, soup or roast. They are a great alternative to bread or bread rolls. Add diced bacon to the dough for an even more savoury muffin flavour, if you like.

Preheat the oven to 190°C (375°F/Gas mark 5) and line 8 holes in a muffin tin with paper cup liners. Melt the butter and grate the parmesan finely.

Combine the cornmeal, flour, polenta, cream of tartar powder, salt and cayenne pepper in a mixing bowl. Stir in 80 g (2¾ oz) grated parmesan. Make a well in the middle of the dry ingredients. Pour in the melted, cooled butter, lightly beaten egg and milk. Stir all ingredients to combine.

Fill the paper cup liners about three quarters with dough and sprinkle the muffins with the remaining parmesan and sesame seeds. Bake in the preheated oven for about 20–22 minutes until golden brown. Remove from the muffin tin and leave to cool.

INGREDIENTS

Makes 8

60 g (2¼ oz) butter
90 g (3¼ oz) parmesan, finely grated
100 g (3½ oz) cornmeal
80 g (2¾ oz) flour
40 g (1½ oz) polenta
3 tsp cream of tartar powder
1 pinch salt
¼ tsp cayenne pepper
1 egg
180 ml (6 fl oz/¾ cup) milk

Also:
About 8 tsp sesame seeds for sprinkling

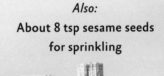

THE
Bakeshop

Hot Drinks

	8 oz	12 oz	16 oz
BREWED COFFEE		2.00	2.25
AMERICANO		2.75	3.00
CAPPUCCINO	3.50	4.00	4.25
LATTE	3.50	4.00	4.25
HOT CHOCOLATE		3.75	4.25
MOCHA		4.25	4.75
CHAI LATTE		3.75	4.25
TEA		2.00	2.25
HOT APPLE CIDER		2.75	3.25

	single	double
ESPRESSO	2.10	2.50
MACHIATO	2.75	3.00

Cold Drinks 16 oz

ICED AMERICANO	3.75	ICED TEA	3.25
ICED BREWED	3.00	ICED CHAI	4.25
ICED CAPPUCCINO	4.25	COLD APPLE	
ICED LATTE	4.00	CIDER 12 oz	3.50

EXTRA SHOT of ESPRESSO
75 ¢

SOY MILK
60 ¢

Macarons

1 $2.50	6 $16.00	12 $32.00

EMERGENCY CARE FOR
CHOKING

Sandwich
Menu

Ham & Cheese
Croissant

Mozzarella,
Olive Tapenade,
Tomato & Arugula

Prosciutto,
Manchego Cheese,
& Tomato

Goat Cheese,
Roasted Vegetables
& Arugula

Gouda,
Tomato
& Cucumber

BAGELS

Whether sprinkled with poppy seeds or sesame seeds, whether sweet or savoury – these yeasted bread rings have a long tradition. Bagels are traditional Eastern European breads that were brought to the USA by immigrants. These days, they are as much a fixture of American life as the *New York Times*. Bagels are briefly boiled before they are baked with steam to give them their typical, shiny crust.

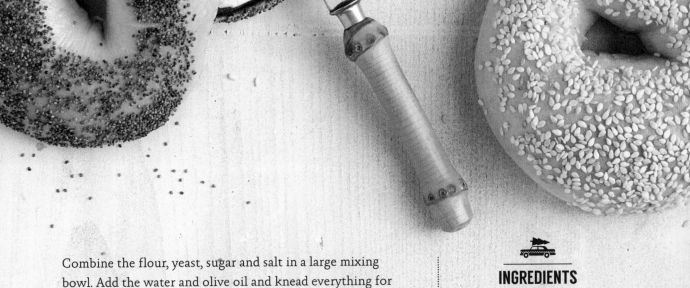

Combine the flour, yeast, sugar and salt in a large mixing bowl. Add the water and olive oil and knead everything for about 8 minutes to make a smooth, pliable dough. Cover the bowl with cling wrap and leave the dough to rise in a warm spot for about 1 hour.

Dust the dough with flour and remove it from the bowl. Dust your benchtop with flour and knead the dough briefly, then shape it into a thick sausage. Divide the dough into 8 even portions and shape each portion into a round. Dust the handle of a wooden spoon with flour and use it to make a hole in the centre of each dough round. Widen the hole to about 3 cm (1¼ inches). Dust the bagels with a little flour on both sides, cover and leave to rise for another 30 minutes.

Make sure to preheat the oven in time to 200°C (400°F/Gas mark 6). Place a small bowl of water on the bottom of the oven and line two baking trays with baking paper. Bring plenty of water to a boil in a large, wide saucepan. Stir in the honey and salt, then reduce the temperature somewhat. Carefully place the bagels into the simmering water, one at a time, using a large skimmer. Simmer for about 30–40 seconds, then flip them over and cook for another 30–40 seconds. Drain the bagels and transfer them to the baking trays. Whisk the egg with 2 tablespoons water and brush the bagels with the mixture, then sprinkle with poppy seeds, sesame seeds or pistachios.

Slide the trays into the oven and bake the bagels for about 20 minutes or until golden brown. Remove the bowl of water after 10 minutes. Set the bagels aside to cool on a rack.

INGREDIENTS

Makes 8

500 g (1 lb 2 oz) flour
2 tsp dried yeast
1 tbsp sugar
1 tsp salt
250 ml (9 fl oz/1 cup)
lukewarm water
2 tbsp olive oil

Also:
Flour for dusting
1 tbsp honey
1 tsp salt
1 egg
Poppy seeds, sesame seeds and
chopped pistachios for sprinkling

THREE KINDS OF BAGEL FILLINGS

INGREDIENTS

Makes 4 bagels each

For the goat's cheese filling:
4 pistachio bagels
4 tbsp butter, softened
160 g (5¾ oz) soft goat's cheese
4 tsp honey
2 handfuls of rocket

For the smoked salmon filling:
4 poppy seed bagels
4 tbsp butter, softened
4 sprigs dill
1 small red onion
160 g (5¾ oz/⅔ cup)
cream cheese
Horseradish, finely-grated,
to taste
Salt, pepper
2 dashes lemon juice
4 slices smoked salmon
4 leaves iceberg lettuce

For the pastrami filling:
4 sesame bagels
4 tbsp butter, softened
8 small pickled cucumbers
4 tsp hot mustard
200 g (7 oz) pastrami
(alternatively dry-cured ham)
4 leaves oak leaf lettuce
4 tsp mayonnaise
(see recipe on p. 120)

For the goat's cheese filling:
Slice pistachio bagels horizontally and spread each half with butter. Heat a large frying pan and briefly toast the cut, buttered sides of the bagels.

Spread the bagel bottoms with soft goat's cheese and drizzle with 1 teaspoon honey each. Divide the rocket among the bagel halves and top with the bagel tops.

For the smoked salmon filling:
Slice poppy seed bagels horizontally and spread each half with butter. Heat a large frying pan and briefly toast the cut, buttered sides of the bagels.

Rinse the dill, shake off excess water and chop finely. Peel and finely dice the onion. Stir the chopped dill, diced onion and horseradish into the cream cheese to combine. Season the mixture with salt, pepper and lemon juice.

Top the bagel bottoms with 1 slice smoked salmon and a lettuce leaf each. Generously spread the top halves with the cream cheese mixture and assemble the two halves.

For the pastrami filling:
Slice sesame seed bagels horizontally and spread each half with butter. Heat a large frying pan and briefly toast the cut, buttered sides of the bagels.

Slice the pickled cucumbers lengthwise. Spread the bagel bottoms with 1 teaspoon mustard each and top with 50 g pastrami (1¾ oz) each. Top with pickle slices and 1 large lettuce leaf. Spread the top halves with mayonnaise and assemble the two halves.

CHOCOLATE BABKA

If you like your babka very sweet and moist, brush with sugar syrup after baking. To make the syrup, heat 100 g (3½ oz) sugar and 60 ml (¼ cup) water in a small saucepan. Briefly bring to a boil and set aside. Brush the babka with the syrup as soon as it comes out of the oven, then leave to cool a little.

For the dough, combine the flour, yeast, sugar and salt in a mixing bowl. Add the eggs, milk and butter and knead everything for about 10 minutes to make a smooth, pliable dough. Cover the bowl with cling wrap and leave the dough to rise for about 1 hour.

Meanwhile, for the filling, dry-roast the hazelnuts in a small frying pan. Add the sugar and caramelise lightly. Combine the semi-sweet chocolate and butter and melt over a double boiler. Set aside to cool, then stir in the icing sugar and cocoa powder.

Butter the loaf tin. Dust your benchtop with flour and roll the dough out to a rectangle about 35 x 25 cm (14 x 10 inches) size. Spread the chocolate filling evenly across the dough, leaving a margin of about 1.5 cm (⅝ inch). Sprinkle with the caramelised nuts, then roll up the dough tightly and evenly, starting from the narrow side. Halve the rolled-up dough lengthwise with a sharp knife to allow the layers of dough and filling to fan out decoratively. Pinch the ends together and carefully intertwine the two strands, making sure that the cut surfaces always point upwards. Transfer the intertwined dough roll to the loaf tin, cover and set aside to rise for another hour.

Make sure to preheat the oven in time to 175°C (330°F/Gas mark 4-5). Bake the babka for 30–35 minutes. If the surface gets too dark, cover the loaf with aluminium foil after about half of the baking time. Remove the tin from the oven and set aside to cool before removing the babka from the tin. Leave to cool fully before slicing.

INGREDIENTS

*Makes 1 loaf
(about 25 x 10 cm/10 x 4 inches)*

For the dough:
290 g (10¼ oz) flour
1½ tsp dried yeast
40 g (1½ oz) sugar
1 generous pinch of salt
2 eggs
60 ml (2 fl oz/¼ cup)
lukewarm milk
70 g (2½ oz) butter, softened

For the filling:
50 g (1¾ oz) hazelnuts,
blanched, coarsely chopped
1 tbsp brown sugar
70 g (2½ oz) high-quality
semi-sweet chocolate
(70% cocoa)
50 g (1¾ oz) butter
25 g (1 oz) icing sugar
(confectioner's sugar)
2 tbsp cocoa powder

Also:
Butter for the tin
Flour for dusting the
work surface

SANDWICHES AND SNACKS

TRADITIONAL SANDWICHES

Black Forest Ham, Emmental, Cucumbers,
Watercress & Apfel Butter on Ciabatta 11.50

Cambozola, Apple, & MicroGreens w.
Honey Shallot Vin. on Walnut Cranberry 10.25

Bologne, Tomato, Bibb Lettuce w. Stone
Ground Mustard on Kaiser Roll 10.00

Black Forest Ham, Smoked Gouda, Pear &
German Mustard on Multigrain 11.50

Egg Salad, Pickles, Dill & Sweet
Mustard on Four Seasons Roll 9.75

OPEN FACED

Smoked Salmon, Radishes, Apple, Dill
& Horseradish Spread on German Rye 12.50

Herring, Boiled Potato, Red Onion &
Cucumber Salat on German Table Bread 10.50

Cambozola, Pear & Red Onion
on German Rye 9.50

Jadawurst, Limburger, Bibb Lettuce &
Red Onion w. German Mustard on
Italian Country 11.50

QUICHE LORRAINE
Served with mixed greens
& Sherry Vinaigrette 10.95

SCHNITZEL
Served with Mixed Greens
& Swabian Potato Salat 10.50

SOUP OF THE DAY
Served with table bread

CHEESE BRETT
Assorted German Cheeses w.
Horseradish, Cornichons, Radish,
& Apfel Butter. Served w.
German Table Bread 12.00

SIDES
Swabian Potato 4.00
Carrot Salat 4.00
German Kraut 4.00
Cucumber Salat 4.00

BROTS AND ROLLS

Landbrot - German Rye 6.00
Multigrain 6.50
Italian Country 4.50
White 4.50
Whole Wheat 4.50
Berlin Brot . . . . ¼ - 3.50 / Whole - 12.00
Müller Brot 7.00
German Table Brot 5.50
Baguette - White 2.50
Baguette - Whole Wheat 3.25
Ciabatta 4.50
Ciabatta Olive 5.50
Walnut Cranberry 7.00

ROLLS

Kaiser . . . 1.50
Multigrain . . . 1.50
Salt Sticks . . . 1.75
Swiss . . . 1.50
Ciabatta . . . 1.50
Rye . . . 1.50
Foccacia . . . 1.50

DAILY BROT

MON. . . . ONION
TUES. . . . FOUR SEASONS
WED. . . . PURE RYE
THUR. . . . COUNTRY SPICE
FRI. . . . POTATO
SAT. . . . MOUNTAIN LOAF
SUN. . . . KHORASAN

SAVORY

FLAMING PIE
Baked Alsation Bread Dough
w. Creme Fraiche, Bacon & Onion
. . . . $12.00

BRATS AND DOGS
Served with bread roll, Sauer
German Mustard & Ptom Ketch

FARMERS BRAT
$8.00

NUREMBURGER BRAT
$8.00

ANDOUILLE SAUSAGE
$9.00

OLD-FASHION FRANKFURT
$7.50

FRANKFURTER ROL
$4.50

MINI CINNAMON SCROLLS

On any stroll through New York's streets, there's often an enticing smell of freshly baked cinnamon scrolls coming out of cafés. These frosted pastries are a fixture of American coffee culture and just the thing for sweetening a cold winter's day while you warm up with a steaming cup of tea or cappuccino.

INGREDIENTS

*Makes 1 tin
(about 16 x 25 cm/6¼ x 10 inches)
or about 12 scrolls*

For the dough:
250 g (9 oz) flour
1 tsp dried yeast
1 pinch salt
15 g (½ oz) brown sugar
1 tsp vanilla sugar
100 ml (3½ fl oz) lukewarm milk
25 g (1 oz) butter, melted
1 egg

For the filling:
50 g butter, melted
30 g sugar
2 tsp cinnamon
1 pinch ground nutmeg

For the frosting:
50 g (1¾ oz) icing sugar
(confectioner's sugar)
70 g (2½ oz) cream cheese
15 ml (½ fl oz) lukewarm milk

Also:
Flour for dusting the
work surface
Butter for the tin
Milk for brushing

For the dough, combine the flour, yeast, salt, sugar and vanilla sugar in a mixing bowl. Add the milk, butter and egg and knead everything for about 5 minutes to make a smooth, pliable dough. Cover the bowl with cling wrap and leave the dough to rise for about 1½ hours.

Dust your benchtop with flour and roll the dough out to a thin rectangle about 25 x 35 cm (10 x 14 inches) in size. Generously spread with melted butter, making sure to cover the dough all the way to the edges. Combine the sugar, cinnamon and ground nutmeg in a bowl, then sprinkle the mixture evenly on the butter, leaving a little margin. Roll the dough up from the long side and cut into 12 even slices about 2.5 cm (1 inch) thick. Place the scrolls in a buttered tin, leaving about 1–1.5 cm (½-⅝ inch) space between them. Cover with cling wrap and leave to rise for another 30 minutes.

Make sure to preheat the oven in time to 175°C (330°F/Gas mark 4-5). Brush the cinnamon scrolls with milk and bake until golden brown, about 25–30 minutes. Meanwhile, combine the icing sugar, cream cheese and milk to make the frosting. Cover the scrolls with the frosting as soon as they come out of the oven. Serve warm.

BLINTZES WITH QUARK FILLING

These thin, filled pancakes originally come from Eastern Europe and were introduced to the United States by Jewish immigrants. They are often simply spread with butter, but you can also add savoury or sweet fillings to taste, such as honey, quark, minced meat or cheese. Our quark blintzes are particularly delicious with stewed blueberries. An irresistible treat that will vanish off the table in the blintz of an eye!

For the batter, melt the butter and set aside to cool to room temperature. Whisk the eggs with milk and melted butter. Combine the flour, salt and sugar in a mixing bowl, then gradually stir in the milk and egg mixture. Keep stirring to make a smooth batter. Cover and set aside to rest for about 45 minutes.

Meanwhile, combine the quark, egg, flour, maple syrup, vanilla sugar and cinnamon for the filling.

Heat a non-stick pan and melt a little butter. Add 1–2 small ladlefuls of batter (depending on the size of the pan) and swirl the pan to coat the entire base with a thin layer of batter. Bake the blintzes over medium heat until golden. Cook on one side only – this should only take a few minutes. Set aside the cooked blintzes on a plate. Keep baking the blintzes until you have used up all of the batter (makes about 6–8).

Lay the blintzes out with the cooked side on top. Place 1–2 tablespoons of the quark filling in the centre of the bottom half of each blintz. Fold the blintzes up from the bottom towards the centre. Fold both sides in towards the centre and finally fold in the top to make a neat parcel. Heat the frying pan over low to medium heat and melt a little butter. Add the blintzes and fry until the filling has set and the outside has turned a beautiful golden brown, about 5 minutes per side. Serve the blintzes with maple syrup or honey, icing sugar or jam.

INGREDIENTS

*Makes about 6–8
(depending on pan size)*

For the dough:
25 g (1 oz) butter
2 eggs at room temperature
240 ml (8 fl oz) milk
at room temperature
90 g (3¼ oz) flour
1 generous pinch of salt
1 generous pinch of sugar

For the filling:
350 g (12 oz) quark
1 egg
1½ tbsp flour
1½ tbsp maple syrup
(or honey)
2 tsp vanilla sugar
½ tsp cinnamon

Also:
Butter for frying
Maple syrup or honey for
drizzling, icing sugar
(confectioner's sugar) for
dusting, or jam to taste

ORANGE AND COCONUT SMOOTHIE

This wintry smoothie with vanilla, cinnamon and ginger makes for a healthy alternative when you've had enough sweets for a while. If you feel like something more warming, simply leave out the ice cubes. You can even transfer the smoothie into well-sealing screw-top jars or bottles to take along as a healthy snack on a Christmas shopping outing. You won't run out of steam with these golden delicacies! Just remember to take straws...

INGREDIENTS

Makes 2 large glasses

About 500 g (1 lb 2 oz) oranges (organic), unpeeled weight, without pips
1–2 cm (½-¾ inch) ginger to taste
1 vanilla pod
250 ml (9 fl oz/1 cup) coconut milk
2–3 tsp honey
1 tsp cinnamon

Also:
6 small ice cubes
2 pinches cinnamon

Finely zest ½ orange and set aside the zest. Fillet all of the oranges by first slicing off the tops and bottoms and then peeling the oranges. Then use a sharp knife to remove the individual segments. Transfer the segments to a bowl. Squeeze the remaining pith and pulp over the bowl to extract all of the juice. Peel and finely dice the ginger. Slice the vanilla pod open lengthwise and scrape out the seeds.

Add orange fillets and juice, ginger, vanilla seeds, coconut milk, honey and cinnamon to a blender together with 4 ice cubes and blend, initially at low speed.

Increase the speed and continue to blend until you have a light and creamy smoothie.

Pour the smoothie into two large glasses, add another ice cube to each and garnish with a little orange zest and a pinch of cinnamon.

HAPPY HOLIDAYS

BURGERS, SOUL FOOD & CAKES

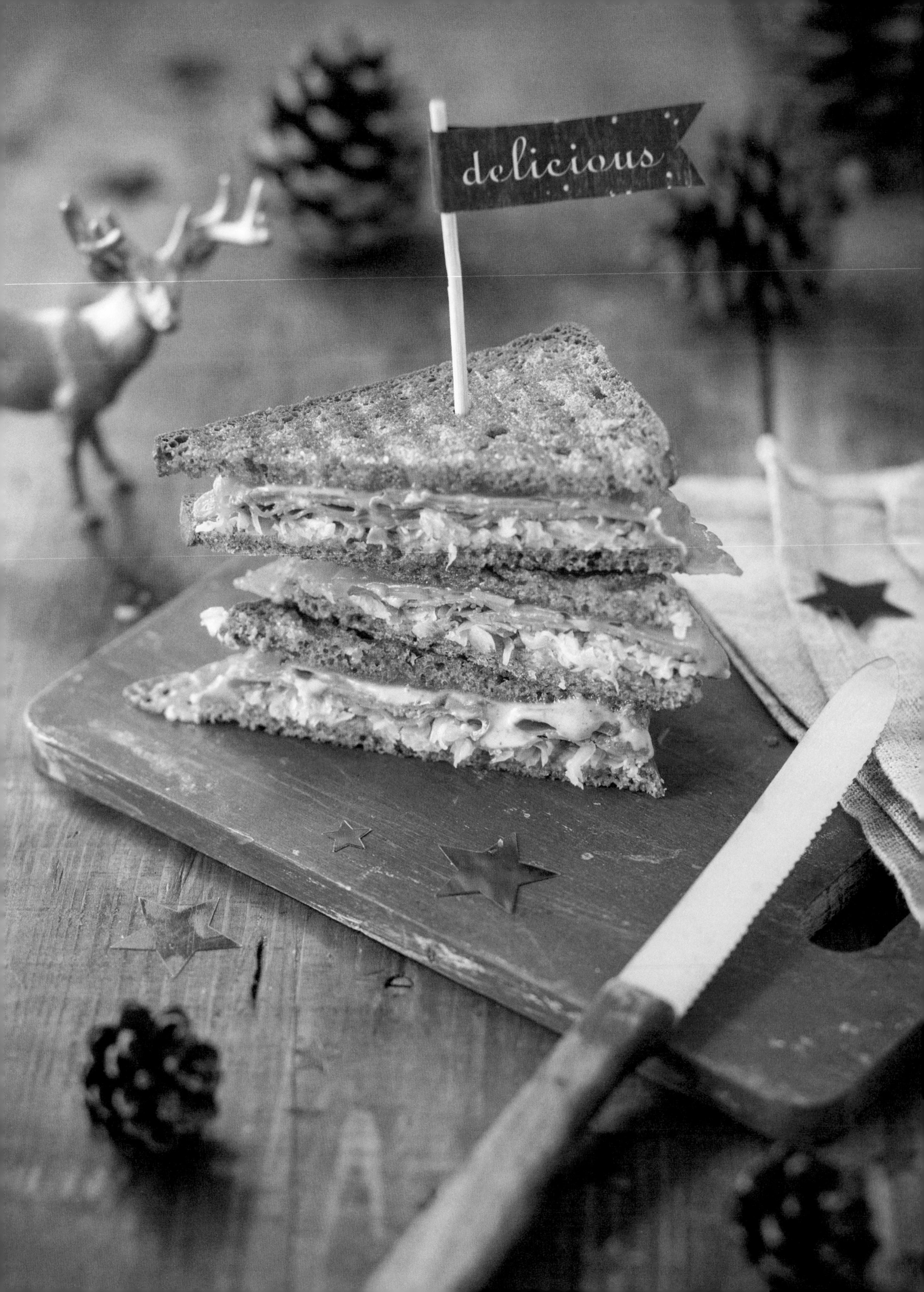
delicious

REUBEN SANDWICH

The origin of this New York classic is uncertain, but many agree that this savoury sandwich was first served in Reuben's Deli on East 58th Street. Traditionally it is made with cured beef, Swiss cheese, sauerkraut and Russian dressing, served between two slices of rye bread. Our version features cheddar and pastrami, which can be substituted for smoked ham, if preferred, or left out altogether for a vegetarian version.

For the dressing, whisk all ingredients until thoroughly combined. Set aside and refrigerate until needed.

For the sandwiches, butter one side of each slice of rye bread. Heat a griddle pan and briefly toast the bread slices, buttered side down.

Preheat the oven to 190°C (375°F/Gas mark 5). Place half of the bread slices on a baking tray lined with baking paper, toasted side down. Spread the top with mustard. Drain the sauerkraut over a sieve. Use your hands to squeeze out more water and then loosen the sauerkraut again.

Top the bread slices with sauerkraut, pastrami, cornichons and cheddar cheese. Drizzle with a little dressing and top with the remaining slices of bread, toasted side up. Place in the oven to heat for about 4 minutes. Remove from the oven, slice the sandwiches diagonally and serve with the rest of the dressing on the side.

INGREDIENTS

Serves 4

For the sandwiches:
8 slices rye bread
8 tsp butter
4 tsp wholegrain mustard
About 160 g (5¾ oz) sauerkraut
8 slices pastrami
8 cornichons (French gherkins),
cut lengthwise into strips
8 slices cheddar

For the dressing:
120 g (4¼ oz) mayonnaise
(see recipe on p. 120)
2 tbsp ketchup
1 tbsp horseradish cream
1 tbsp Worcester sauce
¼ tsp paprika powder

SPAGHETTI & MEAT BALLS

INGREDIENTS

Serves 4

For the meat balls:
500 g (1 lb 2 oz) mixed
minced meat
1 garlic clove
2 shallots
2 eggs
50 g (1¾ oz) breadcrumbs
1 tsp chilli flakes
½ tsp cinnamon
Zest of ½ orange (organic)
1–2 tbsp freshly grated parmesan
Salt, pepper
2 tbsp olive oil

For the tomato sauce:
1 tbsp olive oil
1 garlic clove
1 onion
2 tbsp red wine vinegar
800 g (1 lb 12 oz/3½ cups) diced
tomatoes (from a can)
1 bay leaf
1 tsp oregano
1 tsp thyme
1 pinch sugar
Salt, pepper

For the spaghetti:
500 g (1 lb 2 oz) spaghetti
Salt
½ bunch basil
A block of parmesan
to taste

To prepare the meat balls, place the minced meat in a mixing bowl. Peel the garlic and shallots. Mince the garlic and finely dice the shallots. Add both to the mince together with the eggs, breadcrumbs, chilli flakes, cinnamon, orange zest and parmesan. Generously season the mixture with salt and pepper and knead well to combine. Use moistened hands to shape the mixture into small balls, then set the balls aside on a large, flat plate and refrigerate.

For the tomato sauce, heat the olive oil in a wide saucepan. Peel the garlic and onion. Mince the garlic and finely dice the onion. Add both to the pan and sweat for a few minutes until translucent. Deglaze with red wine vinegar and simmer briefly to reduce. Add the bay leaf and the canned tomatoes together with their juice and simmer for about 30 minutes. Remove the bay leaf and season the sauce with oregano, thyme, sugar, salt and pepper.

Heat the olive oil in a large pan over medium heat. Fry the meat balls until browned on all sides. Transfer the fried meat balls to the simmering tomato sauce. Cover the pot with a lid and continue to cook for about 10 minutes. Season the sauce again with salt and pepper.

Cook the spaghetti al dente in a large pot of salted water. Drain and divide among plates or bowls. Top with a few meat balls and some tomato sauce each. Serve the spaghetti with picked-off basil leaves and freshly shaved parmesan.

MAC & CHEESE

Macaroni and cheese is as much a part of everyday American cooking as the Empire State Building is a part of New York. We have added tomatoes to our version to add a fresh and fruity flavour. Served with a green salad, this makes a perfect winter comfort dish.

Cook the macaroni until just al dente in boiling salted water. Drain, refresh under cold water and set aside.

Dice the bacon. Peel and dice the shallots. Melt the butter in a saucepan. Add the diced bacon and shallots and sweat for a few minutes. Add the flour, stir and sweat for a few more minutes. Gradually add the milk, stirring continuously. Generously season the sauce with Dijon mustard, salt, cayenne pepper and ground nutmeg and simmer until it thickens. Stir in both types of cheese, allow to melt and season the sauce once more.

Preheat the oven to 180°C (350°F/Gas mark 4). Wash and dice the tomatoes, combine with the sauce and macaroni and transfer the mixture to a baking dish. Top with the breadcrumbs and drizzle with the melted butter. Bake the mac 'n' cheese until golden brown, about 25–30 minutes. Switch to the oven's grill function for the last few minutes.

INGREDIENTS

Serves 4

300 g (10½ oz) macaroni
Salt
100 g (3½ oz) bacon
3 shallots
50 g (1¾ oz) butter
2 tbsp flour
500 ml (17 fl oz/2 cups) milk
½ tsp Dijon mustard
Cayenne pepper
Ground nutmeg
200 g (7 oz/2 cups) cheddar, grated
100 g (3½ oz/1 cup) Gouda cheese, semi-mature, grated
3 large tomatoes

Also:
120 g (4¼ oz/2 cups) breadcrumbs
30 g (1 oz) butter, melted

LAMB BURGER WITH POMEGRANATE SEEDS

INGREDIENTS

Serves 4

1 leg of lamb, with bones
(about 1.2 kg/2 lb 12 oz)
Salt, pepper
3 tbsp olive oil
2 onions
4 cloves
1 star anise
1 cinnamon stick
1 bay leaf
½ tsp allspice powder
100 ml (3½ fl oz) red wine
400 g (14 oz) tomatoes, diced
(from a can)
150 g (5½ oz) tomatoes, puréed
125 ml (4 fl oz/½ cup)
beef stock

Also:
4 burger buns
4 tsp butter
A little rocket
40 g (1½ oz) fresh
pomegranate seeds

Trim any fat or tendons off the leg of lamb and rub with salt and pepper. Heat the oil in a roasting pan and brown the meat on all sides (about 10 minutes), then set aside on a large plate. Reserve the oil in the pan.

Preheat the oven to 170°C (325°F/Gas mark 3). Peel and coarsely dice the onions. Reheat the roasting pan and reserved oil. Add the onions, cloves, star anise, cinnamon stick, bay leaf and allspice and sweat for a few minutes. Deglaze with red wine and simmer to reduce a little. Stir in the diced tomatoes from the tin, the puréed tomatoes and stock and bring to a boil. Return the leg of lamb to the pan and baste with the tomato sauce. Cover and braise in the oven for about 3 hours, turning the meat every now and then and basting it with the sauce.

Transfer the leg of lamb to a plate. Transfer the sauce to a small saucepan, bring to a boil and reduce for about 10 minutes. Remove the cloves, star anise, cinnamon stick and bay leaf. Trim the meat off the bone and pull into pieces using two forks. Cover and keep warm.

Halve the bread rolls, spread with butter and briefly toast in a frying pan, cut sides down. Remove from the pan and top the bottom halves with a little rocket and pulled lamb. Drizzle with tomato sauce and sprinkle with pomegranate seeds. Finally add the top halves.

APPLE PIE WITH WALNUTS AND CRANBERRIES

INGREDIENTS

Makes 1 pie (24 cm/9½ inches)

For the dough:
380 g (13½ oz) flour
50 g (1¾ oz) cornflour
(cornstarch)
½ tsp cream of tartar powder
¼ tsp salt
250 g (9 oz) cold butter, diced
100 g (3½ oz/½ cup)
brown sugar
Seeds of ½ vanilla pod
3 egg yolks

For the filling:
5 large apples
Juice of ½ lemon
30 g (1 oz) dried cranberries
40 g (1½ oz/⅓ cup) walnuts
2 eggs
1 egg yolk
100 g (3½ oz) acacia honey
1 tbsp flour
200 g (7 oz) crème fraîche
Seeds of ½ vanilla pod

Also:
Flour for dusting the
work surface
Butter for the tin
Dried beans for blind baking
1 egg, lightly beaten, for brushing
3 tbsp coarse sugar for sprinkling

Combine the flour, cornflour, cream of tartar powder and salt in a mixing bowl. Add the chilled butter and rub together until the mixture resembles coarse breadcrumbs. Add the sugar and vanilla seeds. Mix the egg yolks with 3 tablespoons cold water and add to the mixture. Combine everything to a smooth dough. Set aside 320 g (11¼ oz) of the dough.

Dust your benchtop with flour and roll out the remaining dough to a circle about 30 cm (12 inches) in diameter and 5 mm (¼ inch) thick. Line the buttered pie pan with the dough. Trim off any excess and add it to the remaining dough. Cover the remaining dough with cling wrap and refrigerate. Refrigerate the pie pan with the dough lining for 25 minutes. Preheat the oven to 175°C (330°F/Gas mark 4-5).

Meanwhile, peel, core and dice the apples. Combine them with the lemon juice in a bowl. Chop the cranberries and walnuts and add to the apple mixture. Set aside.

Line the pie base with baking paper and top with dry beans. Blind bake the base for 20 minutes, then remove the baking paper and beans. Continue to bake for another 10 minutes. Leave to cool.

Whisk together the eggs, egg yolk, honey, flour, crème fraîche and vanilla seeds. Combine with the apples and arrange the mixture on top of the pie base in a dome shape. Brush the pie base edges with a little egg.

Dust your benchtop with flour and roll out the remaining dough to a circle about 27 cm (10¾ inches) in diameter and 5 mm (¼ inch) thick. Slice into strips about 1.5 cm (⅝ inch) wide. Carefully arrange the strips on top of the filling to form a lattice. Trim off excess dough. Brush the dough with the remaining egg and generously sprinkle with sugar. Bake the apple pie in the preheated oven for about 75 minutes. Cover with aluminium foil after about 35 minutes.

GINGERBREAD CAKE WITH FROSTING

Decorate this spiced caramel cake with fresh or frozen cranberries to make a perfect centrepiece for any Christmas table. Cranberries are very rich in vitamin C, but their tart taste, which is due to their high acid content, can take a little getting used to. Cranberry shrubs, which are mainly cultivated and harvested in the northern states of the USA, flower in July. Their flowers look a little like the head and beak of a crane – hence the name of these little red fruits.

Melt the butter, sugar and caramel syrup in a small saucepan over low heat, stirring constantly. Transfer to a bowl and leave to cool slightly. Meanwhile, preheat the oven to 150°C (300°F/Gas mark 2) and line the bottom of a springform tin with baking paper. Butter the sides of the tin. Whisk the milk and egg into the butter mixture. Combine the flour, cocoa powder, salt, baking soda and ginger powder in another bowl. Add the butter mixture and combine everything to a smooth dough.

Transfer the dough to the tin and bake in the preheated oven for 50–55 minutes. Use a toothpick to test for doneness!

For the frosting, whisk the cream cheese and vanilla sugar until creamy using an electric whisk at low speed. Gradually add the icing sugar until the frosting has the desired consistency.

Leave the cake to cool for 10 minutes, then remove from the tin and slice through horizontally. Leave to cool fully. Cover the bottom half with half of the frosting, then top with the other half of the cake. Spread the remaining frosting across the top.

INGREDIENTS

Makes 1 cake (18 cm/7 inches)

For the dough:
100 g (3½ oz) butter
90 g (3¼ oz) brown sugar
90 g (3¼ oz) caramel syrup
125 ml (4 fl oz/½ cup) milk
1 egg, lightly beaten
300 g (10½ oz/2 cups) flour
1½ tbsp cocoa powder
1 pinch salt
1 level tsp baking soda
1 level tsp ginger powder

For the frosting:
400 g (14 oz) cream cheese
1-2 tsp vanilla sugar
150 g (5½ oz) icing sugar
(confectioner's sugar)

Also:
Butter for the tin

PUMPKIN PIE

This delicious pie combines the warming flavours of cinnamon, ginger and nutmeg with the mellow, fruity aroma of pumpkin. To make this absolutely irresistible, dust the pie with icing sugar, sprinkle with chopped pecan nuts and, to top it all off, serve with a dollop of crème fraîche or cream.

INGREDIENTS

Makes 1 pie (23 cm/9 inches)
(use a tin with a loose base)

For the dough:
225 g (8 oz) flour
¼ tsp salt
1 tsp brown sugar
125 g (4½ oz) cold butter, diced
1 tsp lemon juice

For the filling:
400 g (14 oz) pumpkin
(e.g. butternut/winter squash),
diced
(peeled weight without seeds)
3–4 tbsp apple juice
2 eggs
1 egg yolk
100 g (3½ oz/½ cup)
brown sugar
50 g (1¾ oz) maple syrup
150 ml (5 fl oz) cream
1 tsp cinnamon
1 tsp ginger
¼ tsp ground nutmeg
1 pinch salt

Also:
Flour for dusting the
work surface
Butter for the tin
Dried beans for blind baking

For the dough, combine the flour, salt and sugar. Add the butter and mix with a fork until crumbly. Add the lemon juice and 1½ tablespoons cold water. Knead to make a smooth dough. Roll out the dough into a circle (27 cm/10¾ inches) on a floured surface and transfer it to a buttered pie pan, forming a 3 cm (1¼ inches) edge. Prick the pastry all over with a fork and chill for about 30 minutes.

Make sure to preheat the oven in time to 200°C (400°F/Gas mark 6). Line the pie base with baking paper and top with dry beans. Blind bake the base in the oven for 15–17 minutes until the edges start to brown. Remove the baking paper and beans and leave the base to cool. Reduce the oven temperature to 150°C (300°F/Gas mark 2).

Meanwhile, prepare the filling. Add the diced pumpkin and apple juice to a saucepan. Briefly bring to a boil, cover and simmer over low heat for about 15 minutes or until cooked. Stir occasionally to make sure the filling does not burn. Purée the cooked pumpkin with a stick blender and set aside to cool.

Whisk the eggs, egg yolk and sugar in a large bowl until foamy. Stir in the puréed pumpkin, maple syrup, cream, cinnamon, ginger, nutmeg and salt until you have a smooth, creamy mixture. Spread the mixture evenly across the pie base to come up almost to the edge. Return the pie to the oven and continue baking for another 35–40 minutes. Use a toothpick to test for doneness! Cover the pie with aluminium foil if the edges turn too dark.

CHEESECAKE

There's nothing like a creamy cheese cake with a fruity topping. You can substitute the cream cheese for just quark if you prefer – both versions of this delicate New York-style cheesecake will taste wonderfully creamy.

INGREDIENTS

Makes 1 cake (18 cm/7 inches)

For the base:
50 g (1¾ oz) butter
120 g (4¼ oz) digestive
biscuits (wholemeal)
1 tsp brown sugar
1 generous pinch of salt
¼ tsp cinnamon
¼ tsp ground cardamom

For the filling:
400 g (14 oz) cream cheese
100 g (3½ oz) quark
130 g (4¾ oz) caster
(superfine) sugar
2 tbsp cornflour (cornstarch)
1 tsp vanilla extract
1 tsp orange zest
(from an organic orange)
1 tbsp orange juice
125 ml (4 fl oz/½ cup) cream
1 egg
1 egg yolk

Also:
Butter for the tin
150 g (5½ oz) frozen blueberries,
defrosted
2–3 tsp icing sugar
(confectioner's sugar)
2 tsp cornflour (cornstarch)
1 tsp orange zest
(from an organic orange)

Preheat the oven to 180°C (350°F/Gas mark 4). To make the base, melt the butter in a small saucepan. Place the biscuits in a zip lock bag and crush them into crumbs. Carefully line a small spring form tin with baking paper and butter the sides. Combine the biscuit crumbs with the butter, sugar, salt, cinnamon and cardamom. Transfer to the tin and press down to create an even base. This can be easily done with the bottom of a glass, for example. Pre-bake the cake base for 8–10 minutes and then set aside to cool. Reduce the oven temperature to 160°C (315°F/Gas mark 2-3).

For the filling, combine the cream cheese and quark to a smooth mass without any lumps. Stir in the sugar and sieved cornflour, then add the vanilla extract, orange zest and juice. Finally stir in the cream, egg and egg yolk. Do not overmix; stir just enough to combine and make sure that there will be no bubbles or cracks in the cake once it bakes. Spread the filling onto the base and smooth out evenly.

Bake the cheesecake for 55 minutes. Remove from the oven and turn the oven off. The cake will still be a little moist and soft in the middle. Use a sharp knife to carefully separate the edges from the tin. Return the cheesecake to the switched-off oven. Keep the oven door slightly ajar and leave the cake to set and cool fully for 2–3 hours, then transfer to the fridge for at least 6 hours.

Heat the blueberries in a saucepan. Add the icing sugar and bring to a simmer. Combine the cornflour with 2 tablespoons cold water and stir into the blueberries. Simmer for about 1 minute to thicken. Season with orange zest. Leave the topping to cool, then spread on top of the cheese cake. Chill the cake for another hour, then carefully remove from the tin.

CARROT CAKE WITH COCONUT FROSTING

Anybody who has ever enjoyed a piece of delightfully moist carrot cake knows that sweet vegetables work extremely well in cakes. Our version contains plenty of hazelnuts and almonds and therefore needs almost no flour. The cream cheese frosting, with shredded coconut, takes this cake to an altogether new level.

INGREDIENTS

Makes 1 loaf (25 cm/10 inches)

For the dough:
4 eggs
1 pinch salt
320 g (11¼ oz) carrots
125 g (4½ oz) ground hazelnuts
125 g (4½ oz) ground almonds
125 g (4½ oz) brown sugar
2 tbsp flour
2 tsp baking powder
½ tsp cinnamon
Zest of 1 small organic
orange, grated

For the coconut frosting:
200 g (7 oz) cream cheese
(full fat)
100 g (3½ oz) butter, softened
80 g (2¾ oz) icing sugar
(confectioner's sugar)
About 75 g (2½ oz) coconut,
shredded

Also:
Butter for the tin

To make the dough, separate the eggs, add the salt to the egg whites and beat until stiff. Trim, peel and finely grate the carrots.

Preheat the oven to 180°C (350°F/Gas mark 4). Line the bottom of a loaf tin with baking paper and butter the edges. Combine carrots, egg yolks, hazelnuts, almonds, sugar, flour, baking powder, cinnamon and orange zest in a mixing bowl. Gradually fold in the whisked egg whites with a spatula. Transfer the dough evenly to the tin and bake in the preheated oven for 40–45 minutes. Take the tin out of the oven, remove the cake from the tin and leave to cool fully.

For the frosting, whisk the cream cheese and butter until creamy. Gradually add the icing sugar and stir until fully incorporated. Spread the frosting over the carrot cake and sprinkle with shredded coconut.

THE GIFT OF THE Magi

O. Henry

One dollar and eighty-seven cents. That was all. And sixty cents of it was in pennies. Pennies saved one and two at a time by bulldozing the grocer and the vegetable man and the butcher until one's cheeks burned with the silent imputation of parsimony that such close dealing implied. Three times Della counted it. One dollar and eighty-seven cents. And the next day would be Christmas.

There was clearly nothing left to do but flop down on the shabby little couch and howl. So Della did it. Which instigates the moral reflection that life is made up of sobs, sniffles, and smiles, with sniffles predominating.

While the mistress of the home is gradually subsiding from the first stage to the second, take a look at the home. A furnished flat at $8 per week. It did not exactly beggar description, but it certainly had that word on the look-out for the mendicancy squad.

In the vestibule below was a letter-box into which no letter would go, and an electric button from which no mortal finger could coax a ring. Also appertaining thereunto was a card bearing the name "Mr. James Dillingham Young."

The "Dillingham" had been flung to the breeze during a former period of prosperity when its possessor was being paid $30 per week. Now, when the income was shrunk to $20, the letters of "Dillingham" looked

blurred, as though they were thinking seriously of contracting to a modest and unassuming D. But whenever Mr. James Dillingham Young came home and reached his flat above he was called "Jim" and greatly hugged by Mrs. James Dillingham Young, already introduced to you as Della. Which is all very good.

Della finished her cry and attended to her cheeks with the powder rag. She stood by the window and looked out dully at a grey cat walking a grey fence in a grey backyard. Tomorrow would be Christmas Day, and she had only $1.87 with which to buy Jim a present. She had been saving every penny she could for months, with this result. Twenty dollars a week doesn't go far. Expenses had been greater than she had calculated.

They always are. Only $1.87 to buy a present for Jim. Her Jim. Many a happy hour she had spent planning for something nice for him. Something fine and rare and sterling - something just a little bit near to being worthy of the honour of being owned by Jim.

There was a pier-glass between the windows of the room. Perhaps you have seen a pier-glass in an $8 Bat. A very thin and very agile person may, by observing his reflection in a rapid sequence of longitudinal strips, obtain a fairly accurate conception of his looks. Della, being slender, had mastered the art.

Suddenly she whirled from the window and stood before the glass. Her eyes were shining brilliantly, but her face had lost its colour within twenty seconds.

Rapidly she pulled down her hair and let it fall to its full length.

Now, there were two possessions of the James Dillingham Youngs in which they both took a mighty pride. One was Jim's gold watch that had been his father's and his grandfather's. The other was Della's hair. Had the Queen of Sheba lived in the flat across the airshaft, Della would have let her hair hang out of the window some day to dry just to depreciate Her Majesty's jewels and gifts. Had King Solomon been the janitor, with all his treasures piled up in the basement, Jim would have pulled out his watch every time he passed, just to see him pluck at his beard from envy.

So now Della's beautiful hair fell about her, rippling and shining like a cascade of brown waters. It reached below her knee and made itself almost a garment for her. And then she did it up again nervously and quickly. Once she faltered for a minute and stood still while a tear or two splashed on the worn red carpet.

On went her old brown jacket; on went her old brown hat. With a whirl of skirts and with the brilliant sparkle still in her eyes, she cluttered out of the door and down the stairs to the street.

Where she stopped the sign read: 'Mme Sofronie. Hair Goods of All Kinds.' One Eight up Della ran, and collected herself, panting. Madame, large, too white, chilly, hardly looked the 'Sofronie.'

"Will you buy my hair?" asked Della.
"I buy hair," said Madame. "Take yer hat off and let's have a sight at the looks of it."

Down rippled the brown cascade.

"Twenty dollars," said Madame, lifting the mass with a practised hand.

"Give it to me quick," said Della.
Oh, and the next two hours tripped by on rosy wings. Forget the hashed metaphor. She was ransacking the stores for Jim's present.

She found it at last. It surely had been made for Jim and no one else. There was no other like it in any of the stores, and she had turned all of them inside out. It was a platinum fob chain simple and chaste in design, properly proclaiming its value by substance alone and not by meretricious ornamentation - as all good things should do. It was even worthy of The Watch. As soon as she saw it she knew that it must be Jim's. It was like him. Quietness and value - the description applied to both. Twenty-one dollars they took from her for it, and she hurried home with the 78 cents. With that chain on his watch Jim might be properly anxious about the time in any company. Grand as the watch was, he sometimes looked at it on the sly on account of the old leather strap that he used in place of a chain.

When Della reached home her intoxication gave way a little to prudence and reason. She got out her curling irons and lighted the gas and went to work repairing the ravages made by generosity added to love. Which is always a tremendous task dear friends - a mammoth task.

Within forty minutes her head was covered with tiny, close-lying curls that made her look wonderfully like a truant schoolboy. She looked at her reflection in the mirror long, carefully, and critically.

"If Jim doesn't kill me," she said to herself, "before he takes a second look at me, he'll say I look like a Coney Island chorus girl. But what could I do - oh! what could I do with a dollar and eighty-seven cents?"

At 7 o'clock the coffee was made and the frying-pan was on the back of the stove hot and ready to cook the chops.

Jim was never late. Della doubled the fob chain in her hand and sat on the corner of the table near the door that he always entered. Then she heard his step on the stair away down on the first flight, and she turned white for just a moment. She had a habit of saying little silent prayers about the simplest everyday things, and now she whispered: "Please, God, make him think I am still pretty."

The door opened and Jim stepped in and closed it. He looked thin and very serious. Poor fellow, he was only twenty-two - and to be burdened with a family! He needed a new overcoat and he was without gloves.

Jim stepped inside the door, as immovable as a setter at the scent of quail. His eyes were fixed upon Della, and there was an expression in them that she could not read, and it terrified her. It was not anger, nor surprise, nor disapproval, nor horror, nor any of the sentiments that she had been prepared for. He simply stared at her fixedly with that peculiar expression on his face.

Della wriggled off the table and went for him.

"Jim, darling," she cried, "don't look at me that way. I had my hair cut off and sold it because I couldn't have lived through Christmas without giving you a present. It'll grow out again - you won't mind, will you? I just had to do it. My hair grows awfully fast. Say 'Merry Christmas!' Jim, and let's be happy. You don't know what a nice-what a beautiful, nice gift I've got for you."

"You've cut off your hair?" asked Jim, laboriously, as if he had not arrived at that patent fact yet, even after the hardest mental labour.

"Cut it off and sold it," said Della. "Don't you like me just as well, anyhow? I'm me without my hair, ain't I?"

Jim looked about the room curiously.

"You say your hair is gone?" he said, with an air almost of idiocy.

"You needn't look for it," said Della. "It's sold, I tell you - sold and gone, too. It's Christmas Eve, boy. Be good to me, for it went for you. Maybe the hairs of my head were numbered," she went on with a sudden serious sweetness, "but nobody could ever count my love for you. Shall I put the chops on, Jim?"

Out of his trance Jim seemed quickly to wake. He enfolded his Della. For ten seconds let us regard with discreet scrutiny some inconsequential object in the other direction. Eight dollars a week or a million a year - what is the difference? A mathematician or a wit would give you the wrong answer. The magi brought valuable gifts, but that was not among them. This dark assertion will be illuminated later on.

Jim drew a package from his overcoat pocket and threw it upon the table.

"Don't make any mistake, Dell," he said, "about me. I don't think there's anything in the way of a haircut or a shave or a shampoo that could make me like my girl any less. But if you'll unwrap that package you may see why you had me going a while at first."

White fingers and nimble tore at the string and paper. And then an ecstatic scream of joy; and then, alas! a quick feminine change to hysterical tears and wails, necessitating the immediate employment of all the comforting powers of the lord of the flat.

For there lay The Combs - the set of combs, side and back, that Della had worshipped for long in a Broadway window. Beautiful combs, pure tortoise-shell, with jewelled rims - just the shade to wear in the beautiful vanished hair. They were expensive combs, she knew, and her heart had simply craved and yearned over them without the least hope of possession. And now, they were hers, but the tresses that should have adorned the coveted adornments were gone.

But she hugged them to her bosom, and at length she was able to look up with dim eyes and a smile and say: "My hair grows so fast, Jim!"

And then Della leaped up like a little singed cat and cried, "Oh, oh!"

Jim had not yet seen his beautiful present. She held it out to him eagerly upon her open palm. The dull precious metal seemed to flash with a reflection of her bright and ardent spirit.

"Isn't it a dandy, Jim? I hunted all over town to find it. You'll have to look at the time a hundred times a day now. Give me your watch. I want to see how it looks on it."

Instead of obeying, Jim tumbled down on the couch and put his hands under the back of his head and smiled.

"Dell," said he, "let's put our Christmas presents away and keep 'em a while. They're too nice to use just at present. I sold the watch to get the money to buy your combs. And now suppose you put the chops on."

The magi, as you know, were wise men - wonderfully wise men - who brought gifts to the Babe in the manger. They invented the art of giving Christmas presents. Being wise, their gifts were no doubt wise ones, possibly bearing the privilege of exchange in case of duplication. And here I have lamely related to you the uneventful chronicle of two foolish children in a flat who most unwisely sacrificed for each other the greatest treasures of their house. But in a last word to the wise of these days, let it be said that of all who give gifts these two were the wisest. Of all who give and receive gifts, such as they are wisest. Everywhere they are wisest. They are the magi.

STARTERS, MAIN DISHES & DESSERTS

CHRISTMAS
DINNER

BEETROOT SOUP

This deep red soup is a perfect addition to any festive Christmas table and, because beetroot is very rich in important vitamins and minerals, it will help you fight off those winter colds. However, if you'd rather avoid sitting at your Christmas dinner with bright pink fingers, we suggest you wear disposable gloves when preparing the vegetables for this soup!

INGREDIENTS

Serves 4

500 g (1 lb 2 oz) beetroot (beet)
4 shallots
25 g (1 oz) butter
1 tbsp canola oil
300 g (10½ oz) potatoes
150 ml (5 fl oz) dry white wine
About 850 ml (29 fl oz/3¼ cups)
vegetable stock
2 tsp horseradish (from a jar)
Salt, pepper
A little lemon juice

Also:
120 g (4¼ oz) double cream
(heavy cream)
2 handfuls of chives, chopped
2 handfuls of walnuts,
chopped

Peel and dice the beetroot and potatoes. Peel and finely dice the shallots. Heat the butter and oil in a saucepan and sweat the shallots for a few minutes. Add the beetroot and potatoes and sweat for a few more minutes before deglazing with white wine. Simmer for a little to reduce. Add 750 ml (26 fl oz/3 cups) stock, cover with a lid and simmer for about another 25 minutes.

Carefully purée the soup with a stick blender. If it is too thick, stir in the remaining stock. Season with horseradish, salt, pepper and lemon juice. Divide among bowls and serve with a generous dollop of double cream each. Garnish with chopped chives and walnuts.

SPICY PUMPKIN SOUP WITH GINGER CREAM

The pumpkin for this soup is first roasted in the oven with some olive oil and a little honey to give it a unique aroma. Together with the butter-soft, roasted garlic this delivers an irresistibly full flavour.

Preheat the oven to 200°C (400°F/Gas mark 6) and line a tray with baking paper. Trim, deseed and quarter the pumpkin. Drizzle the cut surfaces with 2 tablespoons olive oil and 2 teaspoons honey. Season with salt and pepper and transfer the pumpkin quarters to the baking tray, skin side up. Separate the head of garlic into individual cloves and add these to the baking tray together with the herbs. Roast for about 35–40 minutes.

Peel and finely grate the ginger. Peel and dice wthe shallots. Combine 150 g (5½ oz) double cream with the ginger and remaining honey. Season the cream with salt and chill.

Heat the butter and remaining oil in a large saucepan. Add the shallots and sweat them for a few minutes. Deglaze with white wine and simmer for a little to reduce. Remove the skins from the roasted pumpkin and garlic and add to the saucepan. Coarsely mash and add the stock. Bring everything to a boil and simmer for a few minutes. Purée finely with a stick blender, stir in the remaining double cream and season with salt, pepper, nutmeg and chilli flakes.

Divide the pumpkin soup among bowls and serve garnished with a dollop of ginger cream and some toasted pumpkin seeds.

INGREDIENTS

Serves 4

1.8 kg (4 lb) pumpkin
(e.g. butternut/winter squash)
3 tbsp olive oil
3 tsp honey
Salt, pepper
1 small head of garlic
1 sprig rosemary
2 sprigs thyme
About 3 cm (1¼ inches) ginger
4 shallots
250 g (9 oz) double cream
(heavy cream)
1 tbsp butter
100 ml (3½ fl oz) white wine
About 850 ml (29 fl oz/3¼ cups)
chicken stock
(alternatively vegetable stock)
½ tsp ground nutmeg
½ tsp chilli flakes

Also:
Toasted pumpkin seeds to taste

FENNEL AND ORANGE SALAD WITH RAISINS

This fresh, crisp salad with its subtle aniseed flavour adds exciting variety to any dinner table next to a hearty roast and mashed potatoes. Make sure to shop for crisp, firm bulbs of fennel with no brown patches and fresh, bright green fronds. This is particularly important when vegetables are served raw, as is the case with this salad. Also wash the fennel bulbs thoroughly, as sand and grit often accumulates between the leaves.

INGREDIENTS

Serves 4

4 bulbs fennel
Juice of 1 lemon
Salt, pepper
1 red onion
4 small oranges
1 star anise
2 tbsp maple syrup
4 tbsp olive oil
2 handfuls of raisins

Wash the fennel bulbs, pat dry and quarter. Trim off the stalks and cut out the hard bases in wedges. Pick off the fronds and set them aside. Use a sharp knife to slice the fennel as thinly as possible. Transfer the slices to a bowl, combine with lemon juice and season with salt and pepper. Peel the onion, slice thinly into rings and set aside.

Cut the tops and bottoms off 3 oranges. Use a sharp knife to peel and fillet the oranges, catching and reserving the juice in a small saucepan. Set the orange fillets aside. Squeeze the remaining orange and add the juice to the saucepan. Add the star anise and bring the juice to a boil. Simmer for about 10 minutes to reduce by half, then stir in the maple syrup.

Drain the fennel over a sieve and gently squeeze out any excess liquid. Return the fennel to the bowl, marinate with olive oil and the reduced orange juice and combine with the onion rings, orange fillets and raisins. Divide among plates and garnish with the fennel fronds before serving.

JINGLE BELLS

Dashing through the snow in a one-horse open sleigh,
O'er the fields we go, laughing all the way.
Bells on bob tail ring, making spirits bright,
What fun it is to ride and sing a sleighing song tonight.

Refrain:
Jingle, bells! Jingle, bells! Jingle all the way!
O what fun it is to ride in a one-horse open sleigh!
Jingle, bells! Jingle, bells! Jingle all the way!
O what fun it is to ride in a one-horse open sleigh.

A day or two ago I thought I'd take a ride,
And soon Miss Fanny Bright was seated by my side.
The horse was lean and lank, misfortune seemed his lot,
He got into a drifted bank and we, we got upsot.

Jingle, bells! Jingle, bells! …

A day or two ago, the story I must tell
I went out on the snow, and on my back I fell;
A gent was riding by in a one-horse open sleigh,
He laughed as there I sprawling lie, but quickly drove away.

Jingle, bells! Jingle, bells! …

Now the ground is white, go it while you're young,
Take the girls tonight and sing this sleighing song.
Just get a bobtailed bay, two-forty as his speed,
Then hitch him to an open sleigh, and crack! You'll take the lead.

WALDORF SALAD WITH CARAMELISED NUTS

This simple salad has been a popular classic since the late 19th century. It was first served by what was then the Waldorf Hotel and is today the Hotel Waldorf Astoria on Park Avenue. If you are pressed for time, you can substitute shop-bought mayonnaise for home-made in this recipe, but the extra effort is really well worth it. Promise.

INGREDIENTS

Serves 4

For the salad:
½ small celeriac
2 tart green apples
Juice of ½ lemon
Salt, pepper

For the mayonnaise:
1 egg yolk
½ tsp medium-hot mustard
2 tsp white wine vinegar
Sea salt
100 ml (3½ fl oz) sunflower oil
2 tbsp olive oil
1 dash lemon juice

Also:
About 80 g (2¾ oz/⅔ cup)
walnuts or pecan nuts,
coarsely chopped
1 tbsp sugar
50 g (1¾ oz) natural yoghurt
½ tsp honey
1 tbsp chives, chopped

To make the mayonnaise, combine the egg yolk, mustard, vinegar and 1 pinch of sea salt in a clean bowl. Measure sunflower and olive oil in a measuring cup. Stand the bowl on a damp dish towel to ensure that it won't slip. Whisk the ingredients in the bowl using an electric mixer. Start by adding the oil in drops to prevent the mixture from separating. Once the mayonnaise has thickened a little, add the oil in a thin, steady stream. Continue to whisk until all of the oil has been added to the bowl and the mayonnaise has a thick, creamy consistency. Season with sea salt and lemon juice and refrigerate until serving.

Preheat the oven to 180°C (350°F/Gas mark 4) and line a tray with baking paper. Combine the sugar with 1½ tablespoons hot water and toss with the nuts. Spread the nuts on the tray and caramelise in the preheated oven for about 10 minutes. Set aside to cool.

For the salad, peel the celeriac and apples and slice into thin julienne strips. This is best done using a mandolin with julienne attachment. Immediately transfer to a bowl and combine with the lemon juice. Season with salt and pepper. Combine the mayonnaise with the yoghurt and honey. Divide the Waldorf salad among plates and serve with the mayonnaise, caramelised nuts and chopped chives.

PARSNIPS WITH BROWNED BUTTER, HAZELNUTS AND THYME

While parsnips are very popular in the US, elsewhere they often live a little in the shadow of potatoes as a more popular side dish. Yet this root vegetable is not only easily digested, but also incredibly versatile. Plus it is among the few vegetables that are at their absolute best in winter, when they have developed their full sweetness and aroma after the first frosts. Our recipe brings out their full, pleasantly nutty aroma by serving them with browned butter and toasted hazelnuts. Yummy!

Preheat the oven to 210°C (410 °F/Gas mark 6-7). Trim and peel the parsnips and quarter lengthwise. Spread them in a single layer on a tray lined with baking paper. Combine olive oil and honey in a small bowl. Season with salt and pepper and drizzle over the parsnips. Lightly crush the garlic cloves and add them to the tray together with the sprigs of thyme. Roast the parsnips in the preheated oven for 35–45 minutes (depending on size), turning a few times.

Meanwhile, dry-roast the hazelnuts in a small frying pan. Leave to cool and chop coarsely. Wipe the pan with kitchen paper, then heat the butter over medium heat. Cook for about 5 minutes to brown, stirring occasionally. Pick off the leaves of the remaining sprigs of thyme and add to the browned butter together with the hazelnuts.

Transfer the roasted parsnips to a serving platter. Remove the garlic and thyme sprigs. Toss with the browned butter, nuts and herbs and season with salt and pepper.

INGREDIENTS

Serves 4–6

8 parsnips
(approx. 1 kg/2lb 4 oz)
4 tbsp olive oil
2 tbsp honey
Salt, pepper
3 garlic cloves
6 sprigs thyme
70 g (2½ oz/½ cup)
hazelnuts
50 g (1¾ oz) butter

ROAST BEEF WITH BRAISED CARROTS

The essential point about roast beef is simply that it must be tender and juicy. It is best to buy high-quality, beautifully marbled meat from a butcher you trust. In our recipe, we slowly cook the roast in an oven at medium heat. The vegetables are added at the same time, and then there's also a delicious sauce, which is prepared in no time. Serve with a side of mashed potatoes.

INGREDIENTS

Serves 4

About 1 kg (2 lb 4 oz)
roasting beef
(with fat)
Salt, pepper
4 shallots
About 10 carrots
3 garlic cloves
3 tbsp canola oil
2 sprigs rosemary
4 sprigs thyme
1 tsp flour
250 ml (9 fl oz/1 cup) red wine
2 tsp cold butter

Rinse the beef briefly under cold running water, pat dry and remove any skin or tendons with a sharp knife, then score the fatty top in a diamond pattern. Be careful not to cut into the lean meat. Season. Peel the shallots, carrots and garlic. Halve the shallots. Halve or quarter the carrots, depending on size, and lightly crush the garlic.

Preheat the oven to 175°C (330°F/Gas mark 4-5). Heat the oil in a roasting pan and sear the meat on all sides (about 8 minutes) until browned. Add the shallots, carrots and garlic for the last 2 minutes and fry with the meat. Insert a meat thermometer through the fatty top into the thickest part of the meat. Transfer the pan with the meat and vegetables to the oven and roast, uncovered, for about 35 minutes. Baste occasionally with the juice accumulating in the pan. Add the herbs after about 20 minutes. The roast is medium done as soon as the meat has reached a core temperature of 60°C (145°F/Gas mark ¼). Wrap the roast in aluminium foil and set aside to rest for about 15 minutes. This ensures that it won't lose too much of its juices when carved.

Meanwhile, remove the carrots, garlic and herbs from the roasting pan. Wrap the carrots in aluminium foil to keep warm. Heat the roasting pan with the meat juices and shallots on the stovetop. Stir in the flour and add the red wine. Simmer the sauce for about 15 minutes to reduce, stirring frequently. Finally add the chilled butter to bind the sauce.

Remove the roast beef from the aluminium foil, reserving any juices and adding them to the sauce. Carve the roast beef and serve with carrots and shallots in red wine sauce.

ROSEMARY MASHED POTATOES

This classic home-cooked mash made from flavourful potatoes is a pure delight. We have added some rosemary for a special touch. If you like even more flavour, add 1–2 crushed garlic cloves.

Rinse the rosemary and shake off excess water. Pick off the leaves, chop finely and set aside.

Peel, wash and coarsely dice the potatoes. Bring a large pot of salted water to the boil. Add the diced potatoes and cook until tender, about 18–20 minutes. Drain the potatoes into a strainer. Leave to rest briefly to allow steam to escape, then return to the pot. Coarsely mash with a potato masher.

Bring the milk to a brief boil. Pour the milk over the mashed potatoes, add the butter and combine, using a wooden spoon. Season with salt, pepper, nutmeg and chopped rosemary.

INGREDIENTS

Serves 4

3–4 small sprigs rosemary
800 g (1 lb 12 oz) floury potatoes
Salt
200–220 ml (7½ fl oz) milk
75 g (2½ oz) butter
Pepper
Nutmeg, freshly grated

SWEET POTATO GRATIN WITH MUSHROOMS AND LEEKS

INGREDIENTS

Serves 4–6

600 g (1 lb 5 oz) sweet potatoes
400 g (14 oz) double cream
(heavy cream)
(alternatively crème fraîche)
200 ml (7 fl oz) vegetable stock
Salt, pepper
6 sprigs thyme
250 g (9 oz) mixed mushrooms
1 small leek
1 tbsp olive oil
1 tbsp butter
About 80 g (2¾ oz) parmesan,
grated

Peel and halve the sweet potatoes. Slice thinly. Bring the double cream and vegetable stock to a boil in a large, wide saucepan. Season with salt and pepper and add 3 sprigs of thyme. Remove the saucepan from the heat and add the sliced sweet potato. Cover and leave to absorb a little of the liquid.

Trim and slice the mushrooms. Trim the leek, wash thoroughly and slice into rings. Pick the leaves off the remaining sprigs of thyme. Heat the olive oil and butter in a large pan. Add the mushrooms and fry for about 5 minutes. Season with salt and pepper and stir in the picked-off thyme leaves and leek.

Preheat the oven to 190°C (375°F/Gas mark 5). Arrange the vegetables in a large baking dish, alternating between layers of sweet potatoes and the mushroom and leek mixture. Season with salt and pepper, pour over the remaining liquid and sprinkle with parmesan.

Transfer the dish to the oven and bake for about 30–40 minutes (depending on the thickness of the sweet potato slices). If you like a crunchy top, switch to the oven's grill function towards the end and grill until golden brown.

GLAZED PORK ROAST

This dish of pork, beautifully glazed with maple syrup, is known as maple-glazed ham in the US and is perfect for a true feast. It combines richness, sweetness, acidity and a hint of spice for a unique, irresistible flavour. If you like, you can substitute honey for part of the maple syrup. Similar to the roast beef recipe above, the vegetables are added to the roasting pan together with the meat, and some of the vegetables are used for the sauce to give it its uniquely aromatic flavour.

Preheat the oven to 200°C (400°F/Gas mark 6). Use a sharp knife to score the fatty top of the meat in a diamond pattern (or have your butcher do this for you). Be careful not to cut into the lean meat below. Briefly rinse the meat under running water and pat dry carefully. Combine the ingredients for the seasoning and rub this thoroughly into the meat. Peel and coarsely dice the onions. Place the meat, fatty side up, into a roasting pan. Add the onions and roast for about 30 minutes on the middle rack of the oven. Meanwhile, peel and coarsely chop the carrots and parsnips.

For the glaze, combine all ingredients in a bowl.

Reduce the oven temperature to 180°C (350°F/Gas mark 4). Arrange the root vegetables around the roast and pour in the beef stock. Continue to roast for 1–1½ hours, regularly basting the meat with its juices. In the last half hour of roasting, baste the meat a few times with the glaze. The meat is cooked when a roasting thermometer inserted at the thickest point reaches 80°C (176°F/Gas mark ¼-½). For a delicious crackling, switch the oven to the grill function for the last 10 minutes of cooking. Remove the roast from the oven, wrap in aluminium foil and set aside to rest for 10 minutes.

For the sauce, strain the cooking juices from the roasting pan into a saucepan. Add a little of the roast vegetables and the other ingredients, then blend to an exquisitely aromatic sauce using a stick blender. Add a little stock if the sauce turns too thick. Carve the roast and serve together with the sauce and the roasted root vegetables to taste.

INGREDIENTS

Serves 4

For the roast:
About 1 kg (2 lb 4 oz) pork
loin, with rind
2 onions
4 large carrots
2 parsnips
500 ml (17 fl oz/2 cups)
beef stock,
plus a little extra for the sauce

For the glaze:
5 tbsp maple syrup
2 tbsp red wine vinegar
1 tbsp balsamic vinegar
1 tsp Dijon mustard
¼ tsp cinnamon
¼ tsp ground nutmeg

For the sauce:
4 tbsp olive oil
2 tsp pepper
1 tsp marjoram
1 tsp salt
½ tsp ground caraway
½ tsp allspice powder
½ tsp chilli flakes
½ tsp cane sugar

TOMATO COBBLER

Cobblers are best known as a type of sweet dish made of seasonal fruit baked with a pastry crust. They date back to the time when the USA was still a British colony. Our recipe is for a savoury version with a beautifully rustic touch coming from the tomatoes, caramelised onions and cheesy crust.

INGREDIENTS

Serves 4

For the tomato mixture:
800 g (1 lb 12 oz)
cherry tomatoes
3 sprigs basil
2 garlic cloves
4 shallots
2 tbsp olive oil
1 tbsp butter
1 tsp brown sugar
2 tbsp balsamic vinegar
½ tsp chilli flakes
Salt, pepper

For the dough:
170 g (6 oz) flour
1 tbsp baking powder
1 pinch salt
1 pinch pepper
90 g (3¼ oz) cold butter, diced
1 tbsp thyme
1 tbsp basil
40 g (1½ oz/½ cup) parmesan,
grated
1 egg
100 ml (3½ fl oz) buttermilk

Wash the tomatoes and pat dry. Rinse the basil, shake off excess water and finely chop the leaves. Peel the garlic and shallots. Mince the garlic and finely dice the shallots.

Heat a frying pan over medium heat. Add the olive oil and butter. Toss in the shallots and sweat for about 10 minutes, stirring occasionally. Add the garlic and fry briefly. Sprinkle over the sugar, leave to caramelise and deglaze with the balsamic vinegar. Reduce briefly, then remove the pan from the heat.

Preheat the oven to 180°C (350°F/Gas mark 4). Combine the tomatoes, basil and caramelised shallot mixture and transfer to one large baking dish or divide among four small baking dishes or ramekins. Season with chilli flakes, salt and pepper.

Meanwhile, combine the flour, baking powder, salt and pepper in a mixing bowl to make the dough. Add the chilled butter and rub in until the mixture resembles coarse breadcrumbs. Stir in the thyme, basil and parmesan. Whisk the egg with the buttermilk and add to the dough. Dollop the dough onto the tomato mixture. Transfer the baking dish or dishes to the preheated oven and bake for about 20–25 minutes or until golden brown.

CHRISTMAS CRUMBLE

This crumble tastes irresistibly good as is, but if you like you can stir a pinch of cinnamon into a cup of full-fat or heavy sour cream and add a dollop of this mixture to each jar before serving. Wow!

INGREDIENTS

Serves 4

For the crumble:
80 g (2¾ oz/½ cup) flour
40 g (1½ oz) sugar
1-2 tsp vanilla sugar
2 heaped tsp
cocoa powder (optional)
½ tsp cinnamon
1 pinch salt
50 g (1¾ oz) cold butter, diced

For the fruit mixture:
2 pears
A little lemon juice
1 vanilla pod
300 ml (10½ fl oz) cherry or
redcurrant juice
40 g (1½ oz) sugar
1 cinnamon stick
2 tsp cornflour (cornstarch)
250 g (9 oz/2 cups)
mixed frozen berries to taste
(e.g. blackberries, raspberries,
redcurrants), defrosted

Also:
4 small glass jars
Icing sugar (confectioner's sugar)
for dusting

Peel, core and finely dice the pears. Combine with a little lemon juice to prevent them from browning. Slice the vanilla pod open lengthwise and scrape out the seeds with a knife.

Add the cherry or redcurrant juice to a saucepan together with the sugar, vanilla seeds and pod and cinnamon stick. Bring to a boil. Simmer for about 10 minutes to reduce a little. Whisk the cornflour with 1–2 tablespoons cold water until smooth. Add to the simmering liquid and keep stirring until thickened. Fold in the diced pears and berries. Remove the saucepan from the heat and leave everything to cool. Remove the vanilla pod and cinnamon stick.

Preheat the oven to 175°C (330°F/Gas mark 4-5). For the crumble topping, combine the flour with the sugar, vanilla sugar, cocoa powder to taste, cinnamon and salt. Add the chilled butter and rub in until the mixture holds together in crumbs.

Fill the glass jars two thirds with the fruit mixture, then evenly fill the jars up with the crumble topping. Bake for 12–14 minutes. Remove from the oven and let cool until the crumbles are just warm. Dust with icing sugar and serve.

WARM CHOCOLATE CAKE
WITH VANILLA ICE CREAM

This recipe is bound to make any chocoholic happy. When preparing this recipe, make sure you don't leave the cake in the oven too long, as you want it to retain its moist centre.

Chop the chocolate finely and coarsely dice the butter. Add both to a saucepan and slowly melt over low heat, stirring constantly. Remove the saucepan from the heat and leave the chocolate mixture to cool to lukewarm. Preheat the oven to 180°C (350°F/Gas mark 4). Line the bottom of a springform tin with baking paper. Butter the sides of the tin.

Add the eggs and sugar to a large bowl and whisk until foamy. Stir in the chocolate mixture. Combine the flour with the ground almonds, cinnamon and salt in another bowl. Gently fold the dry ingredients and the vanilla extract into the chocolate and egg mixture until everything is well combined.

Transfer the dough to the tin and level the top. Bake the chocolate cake for 20–25 minutes. It will still be a little moist inside with a soft, almost runny centre. Leave to cool to lukewarm, then dust with cocoa powder. Remove from the tin and cut into slices. Serve with vanilla ice cream.

INGREDIENTS

Makes 1 cake (24 cm)

200 g (7 oz) high-quality
semi-sweet chocolate
(70% cocoa)
200 g (7 oz) butter
4 eggs
125 g (4½ oz) sugar
60 g (2¼ oz) flour
40 g (1½ oz) ground almonds
½ tsp cinnamon
1 pinch salt
1 tsp vanilla extract

Also:
Butter for the tin
Cocoa powder or icing sugar
(confectioner's sugar)
for dusting
Vanilla ice cream for serving

IS THERE A
Santa Claus?

Virginia O'Hanlon

In September 1897, eight-year-old Virginia O'Hanlon wrote a letter to the editor of New York's *Sun* newspaper asking if Santa Claus existed. The quick response by veteran newsman, Francis Pharcellus Church, was printed as an unsigned editorial and has since become part of popular Christmas folklore in the United States.

Dear Editor: I am 8 years old.
Some of my little friends say there is no Santa Claus.
Papa says, 'If you see it in THE SUN it's so.'
Please tell me the truth; is there a Santa Claus?
Virginia O'Hanlon.
115 West Ninety-fifth street.

Virginia, your little friends are wrong. They have been affected by the skepticism of a skeptical age. They do not believe except they see. They think that nothing can be which is not comprehensible by their little minds. All minds, Virginia, whether they be men's or children's, are little. In this great universe of ours man is a mere insect, an ant, in his intellect, as compared with the boundless world about him, as measured by the intelligence capable of grasping the whole of truth and knowledge.

Yes, Virginia, there is a Santa Claus. He exists as certainly as love and generosity and devotion exist, and you know that they abound and give to your life its highest beauty and joy. Alas! how dreary would be the world if there were no Santa Claus. It would be as dreary as if there were no Virginias. There would be no childlike faith then, no poetry, no romance to make tolerable this existence. We should have no enjoyment, except in sense and sight.

The eternal light with which childhood fills the world would be extinguished.

Not believe in Santa Claus! You might as well not believe in fairies! You might get your papa to hire men to watch in all the chimneys on Christmas Eve to catch Santa Claus, but even if they did not see Santa Claus coming down, what would that prove? Nobody sees Santa Claus, but that is no sign that there is no Santa Claus. The most real things in the world are those that neither children nor men can see. Did you ever see fairies dancing on the lawn? Of course not, but that's no proof that they are not there. Nobody can conceive or imagine all the wonders there are unseen and unseeable in the world.

You may tear apart the baby's rattle and see what makes the noise inside, but there is a veil covering the unseen world which not the strongest man, nor even the united strength of all the strongest men that ever lived, could tear apart. Only faith, fancy, poetry, love, romance, can push aside that curtain and view and picture the supernal beauty and glory beyond. Is it all real? Ah, Virginia, in all this world there is nothing else real and abiding.

No Santa Claus! Thank God! he lives, and he lives forever. A thousand years from now, Virginia, nay, ten times ten thousand years from now, he will continue to make glad the heart of childhood.

NEW YEAR'S EVE

APPETISERS, POPCORN & DRINKS

THYME & SALT BREAD STICKS

These thin, hand-rolled bread sticks with sea salt and thyme are originally a specialty from the Piedmont region in northern Italy, but in the USA they are often served as nibbles instead of crisps. Baking them with steam makes them particularly crispy.

Combine the flour, yeast, sugar, thyme and salt in a mixing bowl. Add the egg white, olive oil and water and knead everything for several minutes to make a smooth, pliable dough. Cover the bowl with cling wrap and leave the dough to rise for about 1 hour. Preheat the oven to 200°C (400°F/Gas mark 6). Place a small bowl of water on the bottom of the oven.

Knead the dough once again on a floured benchtop and use scales to divide it into 10 pieces of dough of about 30–35 g (1-1¼ oz) each. Shape the dough into small balls and roll these out into thin bread sticks about 30 cm (12 inches) long.

Line a tray with baking paper and transfer the bread sticks onto the tray, spacing them a little apart. Brush with olive oil and sprinkle with sea salt. Bake until golden brown, about 15–18 minutes. Remove the bowl of water after about 8 minutes. Allow the grissini to cool completely.

INGREDIENTS

Makes about 10

190 g (6¾ oz) spelt flour
1 tsp dried yeast
1 tsp sugar
1 tsp thyme
½ tsp salt
1 egg white (from a small egg)
3 tbsp olive oil
70 ml (2¼ fl oz) lukewarm water

Also:
Flour for dusting the work surface
2 tsp olive oil
1 tsp sea salt

GUACAMOLE & EGGPLANT DIP

These lovely, fresh dips taste fabulous with pita or white bread and are also perfect with crunchy sweet potato crisps (p. 156) and bread sticks (p. 149).

INGREDIENTS

GUACAMOLE
Serves 4

2 ripe avocados
1 small lemon
2 tbsp olive oil
2 garlic cloves
2 shallots
4 sprigs flat-leaf parsley
Sea salt, pepper
¼ tsp chilli flakes

EGGPLANT DIP
Serves 4

2 eggplants (aubergine)
Sea salt, pepper
3 tbsp olive oil, plus 2 tsp extra
4 sprigs thyme
2 garlic cloves
1 dash lemon juice
2 tbsp sesame seeds
1 pinch cinnamon
1 pinch cardamom powder

Guacamole

Halve the avocados, remove the stones and transfer the avocado flesh to a bowl. Immediately juice the lemon and combine the lemon juice and olive oil with the avocados. This is most easily done by mashing everything together with a fork.

Peel the garlic and shallots. Mince the garlic and finely dice the shallots. Rinse the parsley, shake off excess water and finely chop the leaves. Combine the garlic, shallots and parsley with the avocado mixture and season the guacamole with a little sea salt, pepper and chilli flakes.

Eggplant dip

Preheat the oven to 210°C (410 °F/Gas mark 6-7). Prick the eggplant skins with a fork all over. Place the eggplants on a large piece of aluminium foil and season generously with sea salt and pepper. Drizzle with olive oil. Add thyme and garlic and seal the aluminium foil tightly. Roast the eggplants in the oven for about 50 minutes.

Remove the eggplants from the oven, take off the aluminium foil and leave to cool a little. Halve and scoop the flesh out with a spoon. Squeeze the garlic out of the skins and combine thoroughly with the eggplant and a dash of lemon juice. Dry-roast the sesame seeds in a small frying pan. Fold into the dip together with the cinnamon and cardamom and season with sea salt, pepper and 2 teaspoons olive oil.

CRANBERRY BUTTER
Serves 4–6

150 g (5½ oz) butter, softened
3 sprigs thyme
1 handful pistachios
1 handful cranberries
Sea salt, pepper

PUMPKIN RELISH
Serves 4–6

½ pumpkin
(butternut/winter squash,
about 600 g/1 lb 5oz including
skin and seeds)
1 large onion
1 small red chilli
3 tbsp olive oil
2½ tbsp brown sugar
Sea salt, pepper
150 ml (5 fl oz) white wine
2 tbsp white balsamic vinegar
2 tsp butter

CRANBERRY BUTTER & PUMPKIN RELISH

Cranberry butter

Whisk the butter until creamy, at least 5 minutes. Rinse the thyme, shake off excess water and finely chop the leaves. Shell the pistachios. Chop the pistachios and cranberries finely. Use a small spatula to combine all ingredients with the whisked butter. Season with sea salt and pepper.

Pumpkin relish

Trim and peel the pumpkin, remove the seeds and finely dice the flesh. Peel and finely dice the onion. Wash and deseed the chilli and also chop finely.

Heat the olive oil in a wide saucepan and sweat the diced pumpkin, onion and chilli for a few minutes over medium heat. Season with sugar, sea salt and pepper and deglaze with the white wine. Cover and simmer for 10 minutes, then remove the lid and continue to simmer for another 5–10 minutes to reduce, stirring occasionally. Stir in the vinegar and butter and season the relish once more to taste.

SWEET POTATO CRISPS

If you like, you can, of course, deep-fry these crisps rather than bake them in the oven. In that case, it is best to deep-fry them twice to make them extra crispy.

INGREDIENTS

Makes 2 trays for 4 serves

500 g (1 lb 2 oz) sweet potatoes
A little olive oil
Sea salt
Cayenne pepper or
paprika powder to taste

Preheat the oven to 175°C, fan-forced (330°F/Gas mark 4-5) and line 2 trays with baking paper. Peel the sweet potatoes. Halve them, if they are large, and slice them very thinly using a mandolin or a very sharp knife.

Brush the trays with a little olive oil; alternatively, and even better, spray with olive oil, as it is better to use as little oil as possible to get the crisps really crunchy. Arrange the sweet potato slices on the baking trays, being careful to avoid any overlap. Brush or spray the sweet potato slices with a little olive oil and season with sea salt and cayenne pepper or paprika.

Bake the crisps for 15–20 minutes per tray, depending on thickness. Bake the trays separately. During baking, open the oven door a few times to allow steam to escape. This will give the crisps maximum crunch. Be careful not to burn the crisps.

CHOCOLATE-DIPPED PRETZELS

INGREDIENTS

Makes about 125 g (4½ oz)

200 g (7 oz) semi-sweet cooking
chocolate
200 g (7 oz) white cooking
chocolate
125 g (4½ oz) large salted
pretzels

Also to taste:
Shredded coconut
Chopped almonds
Crushed cookies
Hundreds and thousands
for sprinkling

Melt the two types of chocolate separately over a double boiler at low heat. Transfer the chocolate separately to a bowl each.

Dip the salted pretzels about half way into the melted chocolate. Place on the side of the bowl to drain off excess chocolate so that the chocolate layer does not become too thick.

Carefully transfer the chocolate-glazed salted pretzels to a tray lined with baking paper and immediately sprinkle with shredded coconut, chopped almonds, cookie crumbs or hundreds and thousands. Leave the chocolate to cool and firm up fully before serving.

CARAMEL POPCORN

If you would like to add a more wintry touch to this popcorn, stir a generous pinch of cinnamon into the caramel. Served in pretty glasses, this popcorn makes a delicious snack for a great party. Start the new year with a pop!

Preheat the oven to 60°C (145°F/Gas mark ¼) and line a tray with baking paper. For the popcorn, heat the oil in a large saucepan. As soon as the oil is hot, add the popcorn kernels. Swirl the pot once to coat the kernels in oil, then seal with a lid. As soon as the first kernels start to pop, reduce the temperature and give the pot a shake every now and then.

Once you hear no more kernels popping, take the pot off the heat and spread the popcorn on the baking tray. Remove unpopped kernels. Keep the popcorn warm in the oven.

For the caramel, combine baking soda and salt. Heat the sugar and vanilla sugar, caramel syrup, butter and 2 tablespoons water in a large pot until the sugar has dissolved. Do not stir. Once the sugar has dissolved, swirl the pot once and leave the sugar to caramelise over medium heat for about 5 minutes. Remove the pot from the heat and stir in the baking soda mixture. Add the popcorn to the pot as soon as the mixture starts to foam a little. Stir well until the popcorn is well coated with the caramel. Return the caramel popcorn to the tray and quickly separate the individual popcorn pieces. Leave to cool fully and store in an airtight container.

INGREDIENTS

Serves 2–4

For the popcorn:
6 tbsp sunflower oil
50 g (1¾ oz) popcorn kernels

For the caramel:
½ tsp baking soda
1 generous pinch of sea salt
100 g sugar
1-2 tsp vanilla sugar
3 tbsp caramel syrup
1 tbsp butter

EGGNOG

This popular drink keeps everybody warm even on the coldest of winter nights! As the eggs for eggnog are not cooked, make sure they are really fresh. In many American families, eggnog is still the Christmas and New Year's Eve drink of tradition and choice. The origin of the name is a mystery, though, as is the history of the drink. But, no matter where eggnog comes from, it tastes fabulous. A very Merry Christmas and a Happy New Year!

INGREDIENTS

Makes 8 small glasses

4 eggs
120 g (4¼ oz) sugar, plus
1 tsp extra
450 ml (16 fl oz) milk
1 cinnamon stick
3 cloves
250 ml (9 fl oz/1 cup) cream
½ tsp ground nutmeg
¼ tsp allspice powder
1 tsp vanilla extract
3 tbsp dark rum
2 tbsp whiskey

Also:
A little ground cinnamon
for garnish

Separate the eggs. Whisk the egg yolks to a light, foamy mass in a mixing bowl. Add the sugar and continue whisking until fluffy. In a separate bowl, whisk the egg whites and 1 teaspoon sugar until stiff. Set aside.

Gently heat the milk, cinnamon and cloves in a saucepan, but do not boil. Stir half of the milk into the egg yolk mixture to even out their temperatures, then return the egg and milk mixture to the saucepan. Reheat over low to medium heat until the mixture thickens, stirring continuously with a wooden spoon. Do not allow to boil!

Remove the pot from the heat and stir in the cream. Remove the cinnamon stick and cloves and leave the eggnog to cool. Season with nutmeg, allspice and vanilla extract to taste and add the rum and whiskey. Gently fold in the whisked egg whites and refrigerate the eggnog for at least 1 hour. Transfer to glasses and serve garnished with ground cinnamon.

BLOODY MARY & MANHATTAN

INGREDIENTS

BLOODY MARY
Makes 4 long drinks

4 small sticks of celery
600 ml (21 fl oz) tomato juice
40 ml (1¼ fl oz) lemon juice,
freshly squeezed
1 tsp Worcester sauce
2 drops Tabasco
1 tsp celery salt
½ tsp cayenne pepper
Cinnamon
200 ml (7 fl oz) vodka

Also:
1 large cocktail shaker
Ice cubes
Bar strainer

MANHATTAN
Makes 4 Martinis

240 ml (8 fl oz) Canadian whisky
160 ml (5¼ fl oz) red vermouth
(e.g. Martini Rosso)
4 dashes Angostura bitters

Also:
Ice cubes
Cocktail shaker
4 cocktail cherries (from a jar)
4 cocktail skewers
Bar strainer

Bloody Mary
Wash and pat dry the celery sticks. Trim off the ends.

Fill a cocktail shaker with 10 ice cubes. Add the tomato juice, lemon juice, Worcester sauce, Tabasco, celery salt, cayenne pepper and a little cinnamon. Shake well to combine. Add the vodka and shake once more vigorously.

Fill the long drink glasses one third with ice cubes and strain the Bloody Mary into the glasses through a bar strainer. Garnish with the celery sticks and serve immediately.

Manhattan
Add whisky, vermouth and Angostura bitters to a cocktail shaker together with 8 ice cubes. Shake vigorously for 10 seconds.

Skewer the cocktail cherries and place 2 ice cubes each into the Martini glasses. Strain the Manhattan straight into the glasses through a bar strainer, decorate with the skewered cherries and serve immediately.

CRANBERRY GIN FIZZ & SIDECAR

Cranberry Gin Fizz
Half fill the shaker with ice cubes. Add gin, cranberry juice, lime juice and sugar. Shake vigorously for at least 15 seconds.

Place 3 ice cubes into each glass and strain the Cranberry Gin Fizz into the glasses through a bar strainer. Stir 2 tablespoons soda water into each glass and garnish the edges with slices of lime. Serve immediately.

Sidecar
Pour the sugar onto a shallow plate. Moisten the rims of the Martini glasses with the lemon wedge and then press the rims evenly into the sugar to frost. Place the glasses into the freezer for 10 minutes.

Half fill the shaker with ice cubes. Add the brandy, orange liqueur and lemon juice and shake vigorously for 10 seconds. Strain the Sidecar into the Martini glasses through a bar strainer. Garnish with lemon zest and serve immediately.

INGREDIENTS

CRANBERRY GIN FIZZ
Makes 4 glasses

240 ml (8 fl oz) gin
100 ml (3½ fl oz) cranberry juice
60 ml (2 fl oz) lime juice
4 tsp caster (superfine) sugar

Also:
Cocktail shaker
Ice cubes
Bar strainer
8 tbsp soda water
4 slices lime (organic)
A few cranberries

SIDECAR
Makes 4 Martinis

240 ml (8 fl oz) brandy
80 ml (2½ fl oz) orange liqueur
(e.g. Cointreau)
80 ml (2½ fl oz)
freshly squeezed
lemon juice

Also:
4 tbsp caster (superfine) sugar
1 lemon wedge
Cocktail shaker
Ice cubes
Bar strainer
4 slices of lemon zest (organic)

INDEX

LISA NIESCHLAG
★

LARS WENTRUP
★

JULIA CAWLEY
★

THE TEAM

Designer and photographer Lisa Nieschlag, who has family roots in New York, loves spending her time in the kitchen, cooking and baking, styling and photographing delicious food. Lars Wentrup is not only the book designer and illustrator, but also a self-appointed gourmet and food tester. The two have run an agency for communication design in the heart of Munster since 2001. A perfect team!

Talented photographer Julia Cawley moved to Brooklyn for love and has worked there ever since as a freelance photographer.

Julia and Lisa publish the trans-Atlantic food blog "Liz & Jewels" together, where they present delicious recipes beautifully – each in her own, unique way. Lisa cooks, styles and photographs in Munster, and Julia in Brooklyn. They have run their blog since 2012 as a culinary challenge and digital pen pal relationship in one.

www.lizandjewels.com

THANKS

Our great thanks go to Julia, who couldn't wait for the snow to come to New York and who ventured out on her photo safaris even in the middle of a blizzard – it was once again great teamwork!

We also would like to thank Christin for her culinary support and David, whose culinary skills we could not have done without.

Tina's experienced eye gave our styling the finishing touch, and Taylor specially flew in from L.A. as our assistant – thank you so much!

Thanks also to Anna and Franziska for the beautiful portraits.

Finally our special thanks to Wolfgang Hölker and the publishing team for their confidence in us and our ability to produce a book across two continents.

A big thank you also to our cooperation partners:
Vivani Schokolade, Royal Copenhagen, 3 Punkt F

IMPRINT

Published in 2017 by Murdoch Books, an imprint of
Allen & Unwin
First published in Germany in 2015 by Hölker Verlag, part of
Coppenrath Verlag GmbH & Co. KG, Hafenweg 30, 48155
Münster, Germany, www.hoelker-verlag.de

Murdoch Books Australia
83 Alexander Street
Crows Nest NSW 2065
Phone: +61 (0) 2 8425 0100
Fax: +61 (0) 2 9906 2218
murdochbooks.com.au
info@murdochbooks.com.au

Murdoch Books UK
Ormond House
26–27 Boswell Street
London WC1N 3JZ
Phone: +44 (0) 20 8785 5995
murdochbooks.co.uk
info@murdochbooks.co.uk

For Corporate Orders & Custom Publishing, contact our
Business Development Team at
salesenquiries@murdochbooks.com.au.

DESIGN AND TYPESETTING:
Nieschlag + Wentrup, Büro für Gestaltung
www.nieschlag-und-wentrup.de

PHOTOS: Lisa Nieschlag: Pages 2, 3, 20, 23, 24, 26, 27, 31, 32, 33,
34, 35, 39, 40, 41, 43, 46, 49, 51, 52, 53, 56, 58, 62, 63, 65, 66, 71,
72, 74, 75, 78, 80, 83, 84, 88, 89, 91, 92, 93, 97, 98, 99, 100, 101,
110, 113, 114, 117, 120, 121, 122, 125, 126, 127, 131, 132, 137,
139, 140, 141, 144, 148, 151, 154, 156, 157, 160, 162, 163, 164,
165, 167, 168, 169, 172
Julia Cawley: Pages 1, 8, 9, 10, 12, 13, 14, 15, 17, 18, 28, 29, 36,
37, 44, 54, 55, 59, 60, 61, 68, 69, 76, 77, 81, 86, 94, 95, 102, 105,
106, 109, 118, 128, 129, 134, 142, 146, 149, 152, 153, 158, 159,
170, 171, 176, title page (www.juliacawley.com)
Anna Haas (portraits of Lisa Nieschlag and Lars Wentrup):
Pages 7 and 174 (www.anna-haas.de)
Franziska Krauss (portrait of Julia Cawley): Pages 7 and 174

ILLUSTRATIONS: Lars Wentrup
RECIPE DEVELOPMENT: Christin Geweke
ON-SITE CHEF: David Görlich
ASSISTANT: Taylor Feldman
EDITOR: Lisa Frischemeier

Pages 10-19: Paul Auster: "Auggie Wren's Christmas Story"

Translated for Murdoch Books by Claudia Koch-McQuillan

A cataloguing-in-publication entry is available from the
catalogue of the National Library of Australia at nla.gov.au.

ISBN 978 1 760631567 Australia
ISBN 978 1 760634209 UK

A catalogue record for this book is available from the
British Library.
Printed by C & C Offset Printing Co. Ltd., China

IMPORTANT: Those who might be at risk from the effects of
salmonella poisoning (the elderly, pregnant women, young
children and those suffering from immune deficiency diseases)
should consult their doctor with any concerns about eating
raw eggs.

OVEN GUIDE: You may find cooking times vary depending on
the oven you are using. For fan-forced ovens, as a general rule,
set the oven temperature to 20°C (70°F) lower than indicated
in the recipe.

MEASURES GUIDE: We have used 15 ml (3 teaspoon)
tablespoon measures.

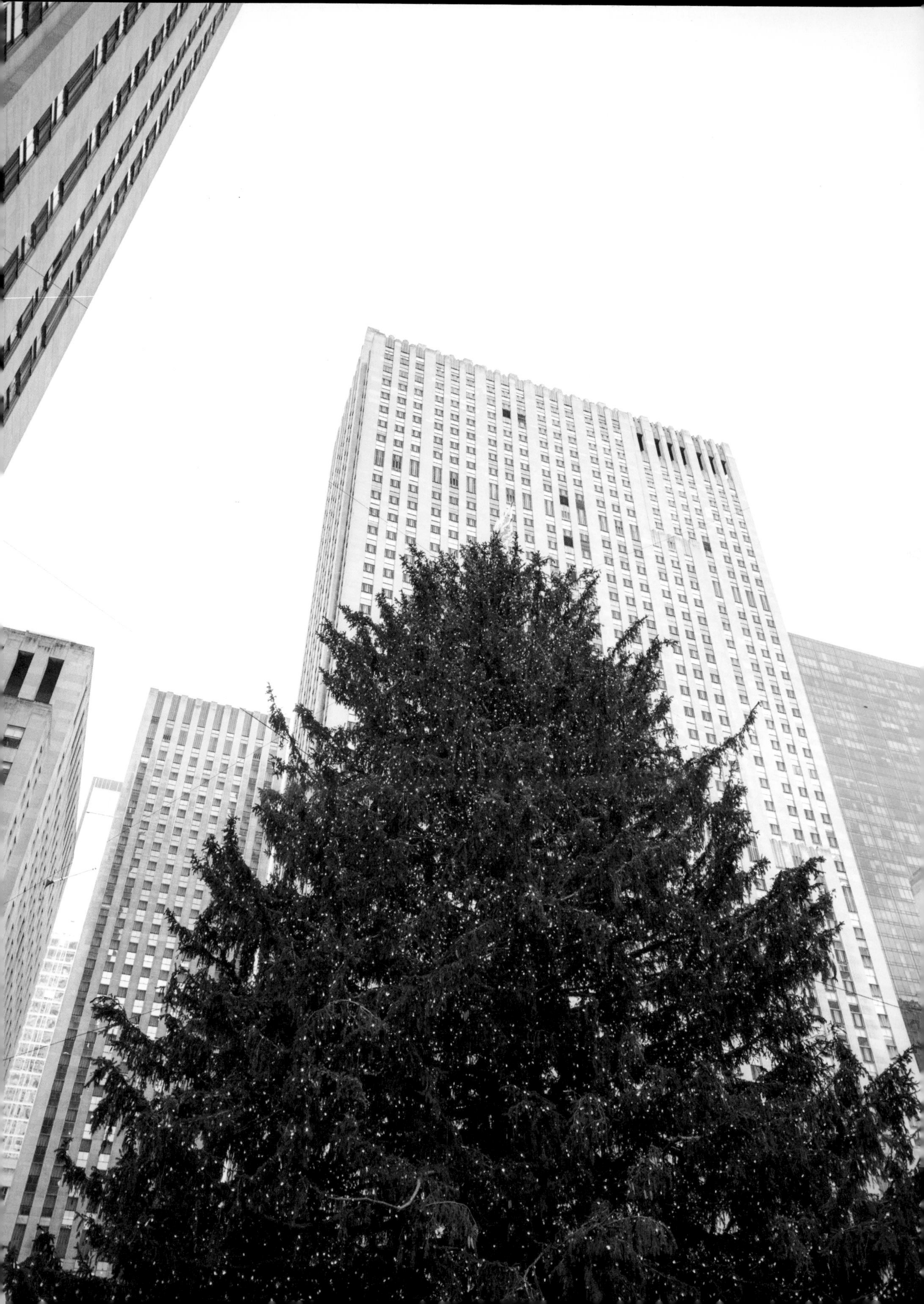